Irene Kappes was born in Hackney, North London, in 1955. She graduated from a major British drama school in 1979 and went on to work as an actress, tutor and director in community and educational theatre. Irene has a PhD in Education.

She became George Pantziarka's step-mother in 1996, when George was three years old and fighting his first cancer. When George passed away in 2011, at the age of 17, Irene began to write George's story and the story of her family's struggle to battle his disease. At the same time, she and her husband founded the George Pantziarka TP53 Trust, to support those affected by the same gene disorder that had predisposed their son to developing cancer.

Irene lives with her husband and their 16-year-old son in South West London; she has a married step-daughter and baby granddaughter.

For The Love of George

Irene Kappes

New Paradigm Publishing

ISBN: 1502741482
ISBN-13: 978-1502741486

This book is dedicated to George, Gina, Viv, Judith, Rita, John, Ian, Ellie, Kane, Verity and all those who have battled with cancer and lost.

For The Love of George

Contents

For The Love of George

Acknowledgements

A huge thank-you to my husband, Panik, for editing the book, for executing the cover design and for technical support in preparing the book for publishing. I can only imagine how painful it must have been for him to read the book, and I am eternally grateful to him for doing so.

Thank you also to Dr Michele Moore for her comments on the first draft, especially her encouragement to use more of George's Facebook entries.

Thank you also to Marilyn and to Niloufer for their comments on the final draft.

For The Love of George

1. In the Beginning

From the moment he was born, George loved life. A small baby, with large brown eyes and wisps of curly brown hair beginning to sprout on his smooth, baby head, he had an endless capacity to laugh that endeared him to everyone. He cried little, slept well, was an easy baby to look after and was doted on as the first male grandchild in a noisy, extended Greek-Cypriot family in London.

He was to grow into a captivating child – beautiful and extremely photogenic. As well as his shock of curly brown hair and huge brown eyes, he had long eyelashes, a cheeky grin and was a very playful little boy. He liked getting into mischief and as a toddler was always to be found waving sticks around or throwing stones where he shouldn't; he loved to be a 'geezer'. He was adored by everyone and was always the centre of attention wherever he went. Sensing how much he was loved, he could unfortunately be quite the little emperor at times, using his favoured position to gain power. Nevertheless, there wasn't an ounce of malice in George and he had an air of innocence that never really left him, even as a teenager.

As a very young child, George lived with his mother, his dad and his older sister, Despina. Although they were all ethnically Greek-Cypriot, Dad, with his darker skin, grey-black hair, black moustache and little goatee beard, was often mistaken for Pakistani, Turkish, Middle Eastern, Spanish or whoever England happened to be playing in the World Cup – usually by some drunken football fan looking for a fight.

Dad had been born in South London and grew up on the estates around Brixton and the Oval. Life was tough and he still had the small scar on the bridge of his nose where, at the tender age of five, he had been launched down concrete steps at school by some older boys. His crime had been not speaking English. He learnt English fast after that, henceforth reserving Greek for home.

Along with his younger brother, Dad learnt to stand up for himself at a young age no matter how big the other boy was. Being small for their ages, it was necessary for the brothers to earn respect in order to be left alone by the bullies. However, when they were teenagers they understood that it was sometimes better to run, especially if the other boys were all white (or all black) and there were lots of them.

Dad spent a fair part of his childhood roaming the streets with his brother, going to see Chelsea play in their second division, dog-days at Stamford Bridge and generally getting into mischief. Otherwise he was at home causing havoc amongst his three younger sisters or getting a whipping from his dad. But he was also a very smart and bookish lad who could argue the hind leg off a donkey. By the age of thirteen, having read the Communist Manifesto and joined a Maoist party, he was out on the streets selling political newspapers or, occasionally, in school arguing politics with his teachers. He left school at the age of sixteen, with just two 'O' levels, much to his teachers' chagrin. He found a job as a clerk at Lambeth Council, became a shop steward and graduated to joining the Anarchist movement, writing for the Anarchist 'Black Flag' newspaper and taking part in the riots of the early 1980s.

Dad met his first wife on a trip to Cyprus and fell immediately in love with her. Gina was a pretty, dark-haired girl of fifteen. A year later they were married – first in England, where they were going to live, and then in typical Greek Orthodox style in Cyprus. For the first years of their marriage they lived in Brixton, on the ninth floor of a block of flats where the lift always smelled of pee and drugs had a high profile.

At the age of 24, just before Despina was born, Dad returned to studying, graduated with a first class honours degree in electrical engineering and found a steady, well-paid job in software development. He quickly earned a reputation as a bit of a geek with a brain the size of a planet (later, in his forties, he would study for his PhD and complete it in record time). Dad was smart; no one would dispute this. He was also super reliable as a husband and parent. He loved his children and would do anything for them. When their first child

Despina was still small, he moved his family out of South London, leaving behind the high-rise flat they had occupied and settled into a maisonette in Chessington, in the South West London Borough of Kingston. It was here that George was born.

George was little over a year old when things started to go badly wrong for the family. Gina suffered from post-natal depression after he was born and began to put on weight fast. Then, just before she was due to go on holiday to Cyprus with Dad and the two children, she began to feel very ill. Her GP assured her it was nothing and the family set off on holiday, but her condition worsened considerably and on return to England she collapsed. It was barely one month after the holiday that she died from ovarian cancer. Dad was devastated. At the time, Despina was eight years old and Dad would never forget the terrible pain of having to go to his daughter's school and tell her that her mummy was never coming back.

Dad's parents moved in nearby and supported the family to carry on. And so young George, who was only fourteen months old at the time of his mother's death, was looked after a great deal by his grandmother. At first he would toddle into his parents' bedroom and search for his mother in the bed, crying inconsolably when he couldn't find her. Gradually he seemed to accept his grandmother in her place and the bond between them remained strong thereafter. Although she loved all her grandchildren, everyone knew that the softest spot in grandmother's heart was reserved for George.

Tragedy struck the family a second time when, less than a year after his mother died, George developed a small hard lump to the side of his left eye. Dad immediately panicked and made an appointment with the GP, who assured him it was nothing to worry about. After having been treated to this kind of dismissive response when George's mother had been ill, Dad wasn't prepared to leave it at that. George was finally referred to Great Ormond Street Children's Hospital, where the lump was subjected to a biopsy and George was diagnosed with his first cancer, on the very day of his second birthday. There is a photograph of him as an angelic toddler in the centre of the picture, blowing out his birthday candles, surrounded by family and nurses. George had a rhabdomyosarcoma (a cancer of connective tissue) in his left temporalis muscle – the one on the side of the face that enables us to raise the eyebrow. There followed a six-month course of chemotherapy after which he was pronounced to be 'in remission' – a tentative suggestion that he might be cured.

Then Dad met Mum.

Mum was calmer than Dad, except when she was really wound up and then she was scary. She was English, tall, slim, with green-blue eyes and shoulder length reddish-brown hair. She became George's and Despina's stepmum when George was three and Despina was ten.

Although her great grandparents had hailed from France, Germany and Scotland, Mum's parents were from Hackney in North East London. Here she was born, in the downstairs of a small terraced house they shared with her grandparents. At the age of six months, she contracted whooping cough and for the next four months infant and parents battled with the dreadful whooping virus. Syrupy medicines were forced down the sick child's throat to no avail, until one night the doctor warned that unless there was improvement by midnight the baby would be gone before morning. The baby, reluctant to leave this world after so short a time in it, pulled out all the stops and turned things around. A couple of days later, her parents spent every last penny they could find to hire a car and driver to take them for a week's holiday on the South coast. They spent the week walking endlessly on the high cliffs and Mum lived to tell the tale. As an adult, she loved the sea and always had a soft spot for Lulworth Cove in Dorset, the place that had finally saved her life.

Mum was the second of two children, arriving nine years after her sister, who, when Mum was twelve, married a Frenchman and went to live in France. Mum's teenage years were at times difficult with no siblings to stick up for her, but she gave as good as she got. She became a rather wild teenager, experimenting with sex, drugs and rock and roll in the true style of seventies rebellion. She had boyfriends that were not approved of, went barefoot to pop festivals and hitchhiked around the country and abroad. She was obsessed with performing arts, particularly theatre, and eventually settled down to focus on getting into a top drama school, which she did at the age of twenty.

After drama school she worked in community theatre and educational drama but, typical of someone in her profession, she was often out of work and never financially secure. Then at the age of 40 she met Dad, who was six years her junior; within a year they were married. Suddenly she had a ready-made family of two; Mum didn't realise how much she had taken on.

Some months after Dad met Mum, the lump on the side of George's face began to grow again. After another period of panic and a visit to Great Ormond Street that provoked another assurance of 'nothing to worry about', it was confirmed that the tumour was growing again. Treatment started over. This time chemotherapy would be followed by a six-week course of radiotherapy and an operation. Mum had a choice to make. Was she going to remain on the side-lines – supportive, but not centrally involved – or was she going to jump in with both feet? She jumped and moved in with the family. Despina often commented in later years that one weekend Mum came to stay and never went home again. It wasn't quite an accurate description of events, but it captured the essence nonetheless. Consequently, Mum and Dad's first year together was spent largely in hospital and it was there that George first addressed Mum as 'Mummy'.

They were sleeping in a four-bed ward at Great Ormond Street Hospital. George was in the hospital bed; Mum and Dad were in a camp bed next to him. Early in the morning George stood on his bed, holding on to the safety rails and peering down at Mum and Dad.

He pointed to each in turn and proclaimed, "Mummy; Daddy."

His sister soon followed suit, although she preferred the name 'Mum'. And so the new family of Mum, Dad, Despina and George, was conceived.

Despina, like her natural mother, was short and slim, with the same dark brown hair and paler skin; she was the oldest of all the grandchildren in the extended family. She was highly-strung and, as a small child, had a tendency to hyperactivity if she consumed too many sweets. She was also demanding of attention from her aunts, Dad's sisters, and she was soon in cahoots with her female cousins – the next two grandchildren to be born.

When she was six, Despina fractured her arm falling off her bed, and it was not her only accident. She could often be heard playing teachers with her dolls in her room. She would line up all the dolls on the bed and berate them loudly and most severely. One day she decided she would have more authority if she could look down on her pupils from higher up. Accordingly, she placed her chair on the bed and this is how she came to fall and fracture her arm. After George was born he was frequently subjected to the schools game, usurping the dolls in their role as pupils, but he didn't seem to mind being ordered around by his big sister.

Despina worked hard at her studies and at school she was not afraid to stand up for her beliefs. She once refused a copy of the Gideon Bible after a visit to the school by the Gideon's, politely declining the book and explaining that she was an atheist, much to the outrage of her teacher who made more than one attempt to foist the book upon her. She was a very organised girl, good with money and generous in bestowing presents at Christmas and birthdays, and she had a strong sense of fairness. Despina studied hard and ironically when she grew up she became a primary school teacher. Luckily she seemed to have changed her tactics and was a dedicated and creative teacher.

There was never a dull moment when Despina was around. She was either ecstatically happy and keen to share her enthusiasm for life with everyone or extremely fed up and equally inclined to display her feelings. She was as volatile as George was even-tempered, and as a teenager frequently took out her anger on the doors in the house. Despite this, home was her safe haven. She was nervous in any new situation – the mist over the heath as they drove through the New Forest at night, the sight of any family member straying too close to a cliff edge, the first week at a new school, having to leave home for university. Her excessive nervousness and her reliance on her father were strangely balanced by her lack of fear in staying alone in the house overnight from the age of fifteen.

When Despina was a teenager there was a good deal of tension in the house, with Mum and Despina especially coming into confrontation. There were probably parallels with many households where teenage girls lurk and peri-menopausal women abide, but there were also added complications. Despina had lost her own mother at the age of eight. Then, at the age of ten all attention was turned to her younger brother when he had developed cancer. Her stepmother arrived on the scene at this point and within months, feeling the need to support Dad, moved in. The changes this brought were hard to negotiate and understandably tensions often ran high. With George it was different. He was younger and more accepting of his stepmother. Being the centre of attention because of his cancer meant he was always confident about being loved; and this inevitably resulted in his being spoilt to a certain extent, especially by his Greek grandparents.

'Yiayia' and 'Buppou' are the Cypriot names respectively for Nan and Granddad and that was how the grandparents on that side were always known. Yiayia was petite, with the family big dark brown eyes and short wavy hair. She was only eleven years older than Mum and had given birth to her first child, Dad, when she was sixteen and newly arrived in England. She had spent the next several years bringing up her children in a number of different flats or council houses in South London, struggling to make ends meet in a strange country and taking on home work as a sewing machinist. Now, her life was focused on her children and her grandchildren.

Buppou, with his cheeky smile and balding head, worked hard as a hospital chef. When he had come to England, he had attended evening classes to learn about cooking and had been employed in several different London hospitals, working his way up the ranks. The first time Mum met him she thought he was very sweet and in later years she still liked to chat with him about gardening and the desire to live somewhere more remote and wild – and to listen to his stories about the past.

George often went to stay with his Yiayia and Buppou, who loved him to bits and went out of their way to give him whatever he wanted. Sometimes this would lead to problems. On one particular occasion, when George was three years old, he had spent the night with his grandparents. The next day he announced that he wanted a 'yeg' to eat. They assumed that he fancied a boiled egg, which he would sometimes have for his lunch at home. The trouble was, George couldn't pronounce his 'r's or his 'l's. For example, 'red' became 'yed' and 'yellow' became 'yeyow'. Mum liked to get him to repeat the tongue-twister, 'Red lorry, yellow lorry'.

To say that George was not happy with his soft-boiled egg would be an understatement. He was beside himself with fury and began screaming that he wanted a 'yeg'! His grandparents were bewildered. They had made him a lovely 'yeg'. Why didn't he eat it? They set about offering him spoonfuls, which needless to say didn't end up in his mouth. They tried to find out what it was then that he actually wanted, but to no avail. George would only repeat his request over and over, louder and louder, angrier and angrier. Finally, in despair, they rang Mum and Dad.

"He wants a leg – of chicken," said Dad, straining to hear over the escalating tantrum in the background.

Of course! George the carnivore, favourite meat: chicken. George, who, when he was older and his younger brother was born, would pounce on the tiniest bit of meat left on the little boy's chicken leg, swiping it off the plate without asking, sneering at the younger boy's incompetence at gnawing a bone. George, who would nag Mum stupid to be allowed to pick the chicken carcass bare, who would polish off six chicken drumsticks in a row at family barbecues, much to Mum's annoyance. George, as Mum said, who would rather suffer the consequences to his bowels than miss the chance to rip some flesh off a bone. And, of course, he got his 'yeg' – after all, it was Yiayia and Buppou.

George's relationship with Yiayia and Buppou was close, but it was his dad who occupied the special place in his heart – both as a small child and when he grew older. George became Dad's friend, the one Dad chatted to about computer stuff or interesting little snippets about artificial intelligence and robots. They shared the same bizarre sense of humour, and even as a teenager George would slip his hand into Dad's as they walked along together. Their relationship was built on a closeness developed when George was in hospital with his first cancer. With George's mother gone, they had been thrown together with the challenge of overcoming adversity, and George was consequently extremely reliant on his father. He loved his sister, he loved his grandparents and his aunts, uncles and cousins, but Dad always was and always would be first.

When Mum first started living with the family, it had been difficult for Dad to go out and leave George. Even after a year, the small, distraught boy would run to the front door as it was closing behind his father and throw himself against it, remaining there, splayed out like some cartoon character from Disney, screaming loudly all the while. Gradually though, he began to trust Mum and would stay at home with her on days when she wasn't working. Like any young child, he could be quite naughty if he didn't get his own way and Mum, inexperienced in child rearing, didn't always find it easy to cope. Despina would try to help, but there was a seven-year age gap between her and George and they also fought quite a lot, which didn't make things easier.

Despina loved her brother, but the huge amount of attention lavished upon him during his illness caused problems at times. Mum and Dad tried to treat them equally, but it wasn't easy under the circumstances and perhaps they didn't try hard enough; either way they didn't always succeed. The first Christmas that Mum spent with the family, George's pile of presents was three times the size of Despina's, which was understandably hard to take for a ten year old. Mum and Dad just hadn't realised how many people had sent gifts for the little boy – aunts, uncles, neighbours, nurses, other health practitioners. Despina was upset and Mum and Dad spent Christmas Eve rushing around creating extra presents for her, to try and make up for the imbalance. Luckily, Christmas day was a great event, with Yiayia, Buppou, aunts, uncles and cousins all coming to dinner. Food had been being prepared for days and tables were joined together for the whole length of the sitting room to accommodate everyone. It was a lively affair and when it was over Despina declared it was the best Christmas she had ever had. Big family Christmases and birthdays were to continue to be a feature of growing up for all the children – either held at home, or with everyone piling into one or other of the aunts and uncles or grandparents' houses on the Greek side of the family.

By June of the year following that first Christmas for the new family, George had received his final treatment for his rhabdomyosarcoma. In total, he had had two long courses of chemotherapy and a six-week course of radiotherapy. Following this, there had been an operation to remove the remains of the stubborn tumour that was left.

It had been a difficult and traumatic time, but George was a resilient child and tough too. And he would demonstrate this frequently during his hospital treatment. Less than forty-eight hours after his operation, he was zooming madly up and down the hospital corridors on a tricycle, with a bag attached to a line draining the wound flung over his shoulder into the little trailer he was towing behind.

Following the operation, in the final stages of his treatment, the histology revealed the presence of microscopic tumour cells extending to the margins of the excision, and George was pronounced 'unlikely to survive'. In fact he was given a five percent chance of survival. Dad was told to "go home and prepare yourself."

Mum and Dad looked at the bouncing, glowing child charging up and down the corridor and refused to accept the news. They turned to Chinese medicine and George was forced to drink a bitter herbal concoction mixed with apple juice for some months to come. Whether it was this, the vitamin and mineral supplements they gave him, the diet changes they made or whether the live tumour cells stopped just at the margins, they would never know – but the tumour did not grow back. Perhaps his immune system had been triggered when he had experienced an infection at the tumour site. Whatever it was, George continued to be healthy and went from strength to strength. The doctors shrugged. Mum and Dad decided that the 'experts' didn't necessarily have all the answers.

Then, once George's treatment was finished, on a bright, sunny July day in 1997 Mum and Dad were married. It wasn't long after the pronouncement of 'unlikely to survive', but George was bouncing around at the wedding like any other young boy of his age.

The reception was held in a hall in Petersham, South West London. It had been raining for weeks leading up to the wedding, but on the actual day the sun peeped through and continued to shine all day. The doors of the hall were propped open at one end and the sun streamed in. Mum had made the wedding cake and she and Dad had stayed up till midnight the night before, cooking desserts. They had bought in legs of ham, huge cheeses and whole salmons decorated with cucumber 'scales'. A friend took on the rest of the catering and there was a huge spread. Buppou was in his element carving the hams and there was plenty of champagne – Dad's favourite. Mum and Dad had set out the long tables with their white cloths, and friends who ran a flower-arranging business organised the blue and white flowers for the tables and around the hall and decorated the pillars with ivy. A trombone trio who were friends of Mum's played music after the meal and, when it was time for coffee, Mum and Dad went round with large trays of hand-made chocolates to chat to friends and family. Despina, quite the young lady, dressed elegantly in a long black skirt and white satin blouse, made a speech. It was a good day for all of them – a good, new beginning.

At the wedding George wore a smart little navy suit with a red and yellow bow tie and looked very cute. His hair hadn't grown out yet from his last round of chemotherapy and consequently he was almost bald and therefore wore a baseball cap with the numbers 1,2,3 on the front. He was extremely photogenic and everyone wanted to take a picture of him, but he sulkily refused to oblige and instead threw off his jacket and tie defiantly, so that he could run around and play hide-and-seek – his favourite game – with all the other kids at the wedding reception. One clever person, however, managed to capture a perfect photo of him, top half only, smiling up to his left (which lucky person was the receiver of this warm, sparkly-eyed smile?), white shirt-collar undone, sleeves rolled up – by some helpful adult no doubt, while he impatiently attempted to wriggle away and escape – brightly-coloured cap firmly on his head, happy and lost in a world of play.

A week later, after Mum and Dad returned from their honeymoon, they took George on holiday to France for three weeks, while his sister went to Cyprus with Yiayia and Buppou, to visit her grandparents on her mother's side. In France they stayed in three different cottages in Maine et Loire, Brittany Atlantique and inland Brittany. In the first cottage they had a small pool, but George wasn't allowed in the water because he still had a Hickman line going into his chest. This was a permanent line that the hospital had inserted under general anaesthetic, to enable the easy giving of chemotherapy and other drugs. Although it was covered with a dressing, it had to be kept dry at all times. So Mum and Dad bought George an inflatable dinghy in which to float around the pool. George would paddle happily, while Mum or Dad swam with him or pushed him around in the little boat. Now and then he would lose his paddle and it would float straight to the bottom of the deep pool, which meant Mum or Dad had to dive down to retrieve it. They didn't mind; it was an idyllic time for the three of them, with plenty of sunshine and rest.

One day Mum took off her swimming costume and ran around the huge garden naked. The house they were staying in was isolated – located out in the country with a garden that was more like a large field. The accommodation comprised an upstairs conversion of a barn, and although there was also a main house on the site where the owners came at the weekend, they had long since departed. When George saw what Mum was doing, he ran towards the barn, where Dad was up on the terrace setting out lunch.

"Dad, Dad, don't look, Mum's naked!" he shouted.

Mum and Dad fell about laughing and George must have decided 'if you can't beat 'em join 'em' because he suddenly threw off his clothes and began running around the field whooping loudly. So Mum and George ran around together and from the neighbouring field the cows looked on at the strange human behaviour.

For the second week they moved on to a house near the coast. George had great fun, riding a pony at a local fair, with great aplomb, and jumping on the trampoline at the beach. Here there was a slight problem though. He kept queuing up for another go and remaining too long on the trampoline, unable to understand a word of the French the excitable young man in charge was saying to him. So Mum and Dad were urged to take him away in order for 'les autres enfants' to have a go. Instead, he played in the sand, or munched sandwiches while staring mesmerised at the undulating waves in the small, rocky cove, his usual happy disposition unaffected by other people's hang-ups.

In the third week, at the last house, George got heavily into hide-and-seek again. Every night Mum and Dad told the story of 'Goldilocks and the Three Bears' and George then had to hide from the wolf – Dad. Each time, Dad would come into a room and do the 'puzzled parent trying to find kid' act.

"Now where can he be? Is he in here? Oh no, where is he then?"

After a couple of displays of this play-acting, Dad would go to where he knew George was hiding because his feet or some other part would be protruding, or he would be audibly giggling to himself, and Dad would act out the wolf gobbling up George. Sometimes Dad would don Mum's shower cap to aid his performance. Mum was never quite sure what the shower cap stood for – a hair net perhaps? But it seemed to help Dad to get into character and was very popular with George.

As George grew older he became more skilled at the game of hide-and-seek until he was always the one nobody could find, but he never grew out of it. It was as if the magic of childhood never left him. He was always ready for a competition and always fought to the last. As a teenager, when he was in hospital with cancer once again, he would play table football with a focus and quiet determination that meant he almost always won. His fiercest competitors were Dad and his Uncle David – Dad's middle sister's husband. They were tough ones to beat, but mostly he succeeded. He just seemed to be able to keep his cool and stay sure of himself no matter what. And he was like this in life too.

Perhaps it was the experience of having had cancer and being subjected to a number of invasive treatments as a young child that gave George his quiet determination in life, his resilience. He certainly went through some tough times, but was always the strong-willed child, a survivor. From his early years his strength of character was evident.

Yes, he was a resilient, stubborn boy. Otherwise how would he have coped – as a small child and in later years? How would he have dealt with the endless interventions, the slight facial disfigurement that was to be the result of the operation for his first cancer, the on-going scares and disruptions to his school life? He took everything in his stride, refused to become a victim of panic, would not allow his life to be defined simply by cancer. At four years old he had survived his first cancer. He now had a second chance and he also had a new family – Mum, Dad, Despina and soon to arrive, baby brother, Louis. Life was good.

2. New Beginnings

After Mum and Dad were married, the family moved to the border between Kingston and Surbiton in South West London, where they occupied a three-bedroom 1930s semi, typical of the area. By this time, George's treatments had come to an end and he was well again – cancer free – despite the poor prognosis given by the doctors at Great Ormond Street. He was now attending The Royal Marsden Hospital, the cancer hospital in Sutton, where he would be a patient in the long-term follow-up clinic for many years to come.

He also started reception class at the local primary school, although he preferred playing on the bikes to doing any kind of schoolwork; but he loved going to school. He would collect up leaves or conkers each day on the way, and on reaching the classroom he would run in calling out his teacher's name in his high pitched voice, while excitedly waving around his latest addition to the classroom nature table.

Despina meanwhile, started at the local girls' secondary school, journeying to school on the short bus route from the house and growing into a young woman, experimenting with make-up and hair products and, like most of her friends, rolling the long, navy, pleated skirt over at the waist, to create a little more fashionable impression. Then, when she was twelve and George was five, their baby brother Louis was born.

Louis arrived in the world after 27 hours of labour, emerging in a most awkward manner and getting his head stuck on the way. He had an endearing way of crying, with a 'la, la, la' sound, except that after hearing it non-stop for two weeks his parents, especially Dad, didn't find it so endearing.

At home, George and Louis shared the back bedroom, initially with Louis in his wooden cot with the rails until he got his own single bed just like George's. Despina had her own small room at the front of the house, next to Mum and Dad's. And so the boys grew up together, sharing their bedroom and their games, either thick as thieves or fighting bitterly, driving Despina mad in her teenage years. George, of course, became a major influence on his little brother's life.

Louis was something of a pain as a baby. When he was eighteen months old he started screaming loudly in the night. Mum, Dad, or both would come running into the boys' room and pick him up, asking what was wrong and trying to soothe him, but he was invariably unable to wake and would carry on screaming hysterically. They tried everything – talking to him, singing to him, shouting at him, once even slapping him to try to break the hysteria – but all to no avail and it would usually be a good twenty minutes before he would finally run out of steam. Then one night Dad took him to the bay window of their bedroom.

"Look Louis there's a fox!" he suddenly announced.

At this, Louis woke instantly and was immediately a model of calm, just a little surprised perhaps to be out of his cot. After that it was always the fox. Somehow, his brother slept right through most of these occasions: George slept deeply.

One night, when Louis was three years old, he came downstairs late in the evening, crying. He explained that George was making this terrible noise and it wouldn't stop. He had tried to ignore it, he had put his head under the pillow, but it just didn't stop. He was very upset, so Mum and Dad were sympathetic and went upstairs to take a look. George was lying on his back, mouth open, a little stream of dribble running from the corner of his mouth, snoring monotonously. Dad gently nudged him and, when the older boy momentarily came to, urged him to turn on his side, which he obligingly did. The snoring stopped; Louis went back to bed and promptly fell asleep.

Louis became the link between the two sides of the family. Eventually, he would grow into a handsome, lightly tanned boy with medium brown hair and brown eyes. Like the rest of the family, he was very slim. He didn't look exactly English, but neither did he look obviously Greek. He became popular at school and quickly gained a reputation as a sensible boy, mature for his age and good at his schoolwork. Although George and Despina were really his half-brother and sister, he never thought of either of them in that way, and he and George were certainly true brothers – it was love/hate all the way.

To Louis, George was an annoying brother. When Louis was little, George explained to his younger brother that only half the bedroom was Louis's and he wasn't allowed to go into his, George's half, without permission. As the older boy occupied the bed by the back window this meant Louis couldn't get access to the window, which in turn meant he couldn't see out into the garden. It was extremely upsetting to the younger boy, even though George didn't actually stick to it all the time, just when he wanted to wind Louis up. The problem was, he often wanted to wind Louis up and always succeeded. Then one day Louis realised that his half of the room contained the door. In theory, George couldn't get in and out of the room without Louis's permission! This really cheered him up. In reality of course he wouldn't have stood a hope in hell's chance of stopping his older brother accessing the door, but just the knowledge that the entrance to the room was in his possession made all the difference. He had the best part of the room, as the door was far more important than the window! Such windings up were to be an on-going feature of their growing up together and would drive Mum to distraction. Louis would complain bitterly to Mum and Dad and, when he could stand it no longer, he would resort to kicking George, which only meant of course that he got himself into trouble.

Dad used to tell them both bedtime stories in that room. He was really good at making up stories. Mum was always at her wits end because they would usually be funny stories and would send the boys into fits of hysterical laughter just as they were supposed to be going to sleep.

In the past, there had been the 'Goudou Goudou' stories told to Despina when she was young, then the 'Dini Monkey' stories for George. Now there was 'Louis Monkey', who travelled by cargo ship from Africa stowed away in a container., the 'Pumpkin Boy', who ate and ate until he burst and Dad's versions of 'The Three Bears', with Baby Bear as a teenager who had tantrums about wanting frumpyflops for breakfast because he hated porridge. But the best of all were the 'Farmer Plonk' stories – with Gerald the sheep, who was smart, Albert the horse, who was definitely not smart and Englebert Wenglebert the mouse, who was crazy. Dad was a great storyteller and everyone was always telling him to write down his stories, but he never did, even though he was already a published author of crime fiction.

When they were young, the boys went to bed at the same time, although George was allowed to sit up and read for a bit, but usually he was laughing too much by then to concentrate on reading. That was the other thing Dad would do – take one of George's big anthologies of stories and change some of the words. They would never know when a word change was coming, but when it did it was so ridiculous that they would just roll around laughing. Yes, Dad and his boys, as Mum used to say.

Poor Mum, she just didn't get it really. Take mealtimes, for example, once Despina had left home, that is. One of them would make a joke about farts or something like that, and that would set someone else off until all three of them were rolling around on their chairs, with Mum just sitting there raising her eyes to the ceiling.

Occasionally in the evenings, Mum would get her way and Dad would do something annoying, like tell a quick story – "Once upon a time... The end." This used to drive the boys crazy. It was funny at first, then irritating, and finally downright annoying. Louis was once really rude to Dad when he did that and got into BIG TROUBLE. He was just desperate to hear a story, that's all. After all, it was Dad who made them want his stories.

Louis also got into trouble when he asked George what the word 'bastard' meant.

"Say it to Dad" suggested the seemingly helpful, but quietly devious, George.

A little later, Dad's eyebrows nearly hit the ceiling as he came into the bedroom and Louis announced innocently, "Dad, you're a bastard."

Poor Louis! He almost always came off worse. When he was ten months old and his big brother was almost six, George nearly drowned Louis. It was a warm summer's day and Mum and Dad had filled the paddling pool, before sitting down to read in the small garden. Despina was out with friends and the boys were playing together, without too much bother, with Louis wearing his froggy water wings. Mum and Dad were peering over their books now and then to check that everything was ok.

George got out of the pool and decided that Louis should get out too. It seemed to George that the easiest way was obviously to drag him out by the feet, somehow causing the baby boy to plop into the water face first. Mum screamed at George and rushed forward to grab Louis, who was still breathing, and of course no harm was done, but mums don't always understand that sort of thing. George was surprised, Dad was fairly blasé about the whole affair and Louis, of course, was just screaming.

Louis got his own back a couple of years later, when at the age of three, swinging a four-foot-long stick – previously a narrow branch of the buddleia tree in the back garden – he intentionally swiped his eight-year-old brother across the back with it several times. Needless to say, Louis got into trouble for that. George, who was actually very honourable, didn't retaliate, given that the boy was five years younger than him, despite the impressive force of the blows. And, despite the big brother windings up, he was always ready to protect Louis from outside antagonists.

In those days, Despina was driven crazy by the two boys. Life had changed very much for her from the days when it was just her and George, when he would do as he was told if she was looking after him. Now, babysitting the two boys was a nightmare. As George got older, with a younger sibling of his own, he was less inclined to heed his older sister's commands. When the two boys were together, to a teenage sister who had her own more grown up concerns – such as watching 'Buffy the Vampire Slayer', secretly acquiring her first mobile phone and listening to music in her bedroom at ninety decibels – it was like living with a pair of aliens.

As well as being looked after by their sister, for part of their growing up, while Mum and Dad were both working, George and Louis were looked after by a nanny, who would pick them up from school and take them to the park, go swimming or play crazy games with them. The boys loved her, as Louis loved his nursery too. They were lucky in the people they were looked after by. They also had a great deal of fun with Dad's family.

Dad's side of the family was large – a true extended Greek family. He had three sisters – Auntie Ann, Auntie Barb, Auntie Flo and a brother, Uncle Mike, plus an ever-increasing stock of nieces and nephews. Family events were numerous when the boys were young. Everyone would crowd into one of the houses for Christmas, birthdays, Greek Easter or New Year. Food would be plentiful, including numerous Greek dishes often brought by Yiayia – koubebia (stuffed vine leaves), macaronia tou fourno (macaroni baked with meat and a white sauce), keftethes (little meat balls made with minced lamb, breadcrumbs and parsley), salty haloumi cheese, elies (olives), koulorin (Greek bread), batichan (water melon). There was always some excuse for a get-together, and it was usually loud and exhausting, with the adults arguing politics or competing for who could be the funniest or express the most outrageous opinions. And all the while, the children would be running around yelling and playing hide-and-seek, football or some other manic game. The boys loved it, as did Despina when she was young. The children would also often go to stay with Yiayia and Buppou and visit their cousins, while Mum and Dad made their monthly trip to visit Nanny Olive – Mum's mum.

Mum's side of the family was smaller and quieter, but the boys also spent time visiting their aunt and uncle in their house in the country in France. They would spend time with their cousin's children, with the huge Newfoundland dog and various ducks, chickens and horses. George, always fond of animals, enjoyed riding one of the horses and in true big brother style, he protected Louis from the dog, who, on their first visit, was actually the same height as the terrified small boy.

As a young boy, George loved toy cars and had a huge collection, which he played with endlessly. He also had a number of tricycles and cars that he would ride madly round and round the garden, graduating to bikes as he got older. His other love was his castle and the knights and soldiers that went with it. Mum and Dad bought Louis one too, so that they could play together. On birthdays or at Christmas time they would invariably each be given a new knight on a horse and they would spend hours in their room challenging and charging each other with them, although Louis had a slightly odd habit of biting the ears off his horses.

George also liked to take things apart and, as he grew older, he amassed quite a collection of little motors, metal plates, screws, wires, all from worn-out toys or some piece of equipment that Mum and Dad were throwing out. He would attempt to make things from them, and for a while they were convinced he would grow up to be an engineer.

Another favourite pastime was playing at war games, first of all in the playground and then on the way home from school, using two fingers as a gun. Mum would pick him up from junior school and suddenly he would be gone, only to reappear the next minute from behind a tree, 'pew pewing' with his voice as he fired at his imaginary foes. Inevitably, once Louis was old enough, he joined his big brother in his combat endeavours and they would 'pew pew' together all around the house, up and down the stairs, behind doors and sofas.

George was certainly a real character. In year six he was in trouble with his teacher, a large, jovial, young woman, who generally found George's humour and mischievousness amusing and endearing. She loved the boy and Mum and Dad felt she let excused his behaviour a little too often and didn't challenge him enough to achieve in his schoolwork. It seemed though that one day he went a little too far even for her. First of all, she reported, in 'sex education' the week before, when she had informed the class that Eskimos had forty different words for making love, George had intoned in a high nasal voice a 'hinhon, hinhon hinhon' sort of sound to complete the picture for the rest of the class. This, she said, had been very disruptive. But this week in sex education, she had had to tell him off severely, when he had put up his hand and interrupted again.

"Which hole do you use?" he had asked.

Mum and Dad could barely keep a straight face

when she told them. Dad thought it was a reasonable question, but Mum said his answer to it would not have gone down well.

Yes, throughout his schooling George loved to entertain the class with his jokes and rejoiced in the role of 'class clown', often to the dismay of his parents. He also loved to win at everything and mostly the adults in the family allowed him to. Louis found this infuriating at times, as his brother would always walk out of a game of Monopoly if he thought he was going to lose. George was often the centre of attention and grew up assuming this would always be the case. It was hard to ensure that he didn't also become very spoilt with all the attention he was given by the family. Consequently Mum and Dad in their efforts to work against this were hard on him at times. They also worried about his health constantly and perhaps over-protected him when it came to playing out in the cold and wet, as he was always prone to developing chesty coughs. They would wrap him up in scarf, woolly hat and gloves in the winter but, like all children, he rarely noticed the cold and would stay out playing football in the damp and dark without a care in the world.

In all, George's childhood was happy, and he was a cheerful, fun-loving child. He was good-natured, cheeky and loved to play the clown. He was also smart, if a little lazy about doing academic work. Most of the time he just muddled along in a slightly air-headed, if sometimes irritating, fashion. He always went slowly and could never be harassed or goaded into getting a move on. At times, he drove his parents to distraction, as it often seemed that the more they tried to hurry him, the slower he went.

As he grew older, he continued to be a popular boy at school, with pupils and teachers alike. In secondary school his antics took a more active form – tying another boy's rucksack (while he was still wearing it) to the blinds or rigging a friend's mobile, so that it would ring loudly in assembly. But it was all harmless fun. As a teenager, he was laid back, but articulate, and probably appeared more confident than he really was. He became interested in the idea of being a businessman and was always on the look out for little schemes to make some money.

He was growing up, but he somehow retained a childlike innocence – despite his increasing interest in pictures of pretty girls and websites that focused on large breasts. He was becoming lanky in appearance, although he was not especially tall for his age, and his shock of dark brown, curly hair was growing more unruly as the years passed. When he let it grow out, it became like an 'afro' and he was able to hide pens and other items in it. It was always difficult to find a barber who could cut his hair, not just because of the thickness, but because he had a scar from his childhood operation going right across the top of his head. Bad haircuts would expose the scar and accentuate the dip in the side of his face where the muscle had been removed. His cheeky grin was still apparent and, although he became less talkative and sometimes moody, or would go into a teenage boy grump, this latter never lasted for long. He was not one to continue an argument or bear a grudge, and in this respect he was the easiest of the three children to deal with.

Then, in June 2008, at the age of fourteen, the bombshell fell – George developed cancer again. His young life from then on was to change daily and dramatically.

For The Love of George

3. How it All Started Again

Between the ages of four and fourteen there were no new incidences of cancer – at least as far as anyone knew. George continued to attend school, and was generally well, apart from coughs, colds and the occasional minor injury. There were a couple of scares, the first of which turned out to be a huge lump of earwax, possibly due to George's glands being affected by the radiotherapy of the infant tumour and causing a build-up of wax all the time. His ears were always dirty and full of wax and it was a struggle to get him to clean them, as he was never too fond of washing. The second incident involved a small lump in the ear canal that was removed and biopsied, but which turned out to be benign. Of course these scares caused a great deal of trauma all round, but they came out right in the end. There were also the on-going check-ups and scans, six-monthly for the first few years and then annually. As well as monitoring for cancer, this follow-up process kept a check on possible side effects from previous treatments, such as reduced production of growth hormones.

George progressed through infants' school into juniors, where school photos of him in his uniform of white shirt, red tie and v-necked jumper show a smiling liquid-eyed, curly-haired boy, whose chin and ears are already beginning to take on something of the prominence they will develop in later years. Then, on to secondary school and black school blazer with the blue griffin badge – school photos were less often taken and more often portraying a jokey George jostling up against his mates.

During this period, Despina went off to university to read psychology, extending her studies to four years in order to complete a year of work experience in the middle. She was preparing to move on to study for a PGCE, with the intention of becoming a primary school teacher. Louis, in the meantime, survived a large number of bumps to his head and moved through nursery into the infants and then juniors at George's old school. Dad completed his PhD and continued to work. Mum began researching for her PhD after she and her colleague closed the performing arts organisation that they had founded and run for several years.

It was not until the early summer of 2008 that the trouble really started again. Just when everyone was beginning to think they were out of the woods and cancer was a thing of the past, George felt a small bump on his head. It was difficult to find, not obvious at all under his thick mop of curly hair, but Dad managed to feel it after several attempts. Even George couldn't always locate it, but he was unnerved by it nonetheless. It was enough to ring a few warning bells and a visit to the local GP seemed like a good idea.

As Dad was at work and Mum was at home concentrating on her PhD, it was she who took George to the afternoon surgery. There they saw a young male doctor in his thirties, who quickly reassured them that the little bump was nothing to worry about at all. However, he was concerned about a small raised patch of skin behind the left ear and wanted to have it checked. He had had a good deal of experience with skin cancers and wanted to be sure George hadn't developed one. He arranged for George to have a biopsy.

The wait for the biopsy results seemed like an age. Skin cancers can sound like a minor problem, but Mum and Dad knew that at their worst they could be fatal. The world was turning upside down and Dad blamed himself for his complacency. Eventually the results came in, confirming the presence of a form of skin cancer known as basal cell carcinoma, possibly caused by the radiotherapy treatment to the left side of George's head 11 years previously. The family were assured that as long as the carcinoma was removed quickly and successfully, it would not develop into anything sinister. This procedure was rapidly executed. Panic over – or so it seemed.

George was on school work experience, for which he had chosen to go to his old infants' school. The skin cancer had arisen during this time and it was unsettling for him, to say the least. George also often seemed very young for his age – not yet fifteen – and he was the youngest in his class. George – fun-loving, mischievous George. Unfortunately he became swept up in the world of children's games – the illegal playing of a game of ball in the classroom; the visit to the junior playground next door to join in a lunchtime football match with Louis and his mates; the sheer joy of entertaining young children who were drawn to him like a magnet. This was not the aim of work experience and he was sent home and almost returned to his school with a large 'F' on his report. However, no one seemed to have explained what his behaviour should have been, what was actually expected of him. Mum made an appointment for herself and George to see the head teacher, who listened sympathetically to George and to Mum's explanation of the current health situation and seemed quite affected by George's story. The head teacher explained what was actually required of him and offered him a second chance, which he grabbed. He was so innocent of the ways of the world and keen to do well. His final report mentioned a ropey start, but that he had turned this around in the end. Another crisis averted.

It was late June and the summer holidays were drawing ever closer, but there was a further problem arising. A week after the removal of the basal cell carcinoma, George began to feel a slight tingling in his chin. Had they caused some damage to a nerve? The tingling continued, prompting a visit to the Royal Marsden, the cancer hospital where he was in the care of the long-term follow-up clinic. From here began a process of to-ing and fro-ing between the Marsden in Sutton and St. George's Hospital in Tooting, where the dental experts resided. George was already seeing the latter for his teeth because they had been affected by the radiotherapy he had had as a young child.

Childhood cancers can have many repercussions for the survivors of the disease. Growing children are often left with other problems and parents and doctors must be constantly vigilant; further surgical interventions or other treatments can be needed. As well as his facial disfigurement, George had dental problems, for which he had paid the dental department at St George's several visits already.

George's jaw had grown a little unevenly – one side longer than the other, which gave his chin a slight twist to the left. This caused problems for his bite, meaning that his teeth didn't meet together on one side. Consequently, there was a plan to operate when he reached sixteen or seventeen, to realign his jaw and teeth. In addition, he was being primed for a decision he would have to make at a later point: he would need to decide whether to opt for plastic surgery, to fill out the dip to the side of his face, caused by the removal of the left temporalis muscle when he was three years old. George was torn on this matter. On the one hand he would have liked to have a symmetrical face – he had suffered from a certain amount of staring and name calling over the years. On the other hand, the disfigurement was mild and he was still a good-looking boy. He had grown up with the little dip in his face and it was part of his identity now. Did he really want to alter that? Although it had become more pronounced as his face grew, his friends regarded it as essentially part of George, and they advised him to leave it be. Meanwhile, he went backwards and forwards between the two hospitals, seeking an answer to the new problem.

The dentists said the problem was not teeth and the cancer doctors – the oncologists – said it was definitely not tumour. The holidays arrived and everyone went away, still none the wiser as to what was going on.

George and Louis went to Cyprus with Yiayia and Buppou. It was Louis's first time there and he was very excited. The boys spent a fortnight basking in the sun, eating delicious Cypriot food, meeting endless relatives and being dragged around various churches on the island, as Yiayia and Buppou were both religious. There were also a couple of visits to the dentist because in addition to the tingling in the jaw George was beginning to feel an odd pressure under his back teeth – but nothing was found. Most mornings though, were spent swimming and diving around in the pool of the seaside apartment that their grandparents had rented. George slept late in true teenage style and joined his brother and granddad in the pool around late morning. Louis returned to the UK with big white patches where he had worn goggles, as he hated getting chlorine in his eyes. The rest of his face was deeply tanned and he looked like a panda when Mum and Dad picked them up at the airport. All in all they had had a great time.

Meanwhile, Mum and Dad went to France, to Anjou near the Loire river, for their first holiday alone since their honeymoon. They stayed in a small gite situated in the garden of the house of a couple of middle-aged English artists. The tiny cottage, with its old terracotta floors and bedroom in the attic felt like a real farmer's abode, but it was beautifully restored and quite comfortable. The two of them spent the week lazing around, drinking chilled local rosé, cooking up delicious meals of merguez with green beans tossed in olive oil and garlic, tomato salads, pâté with cornichons and crusty baguette etc. It was hot and mostly they ate outside in the sunshine, breathing in the perfume of the lavender and thyme and watching lizards run up the walls. In the mornings, Dad lazed in bed writing stories and Mum sat outside eating her breakfast and writing a holiday journal for the children to read when they got home. They had a good relaxing break, although Dad chose 'Schindler's Ark' as one of his holiday reading books, and spent a considerable amount of time blubbing and then missing his boys. And of course, there was still the worry of what was happening to George.

Later in August Mum, Dad and the boys went to Southwold in Suffolk for a week, something they had done since Granddad Charlie (Mum's dad) had died a few years before. They rented a holiday cottage and visited Nanny Olive every day in the little bungalow she lived in further up the coast. A short grey-haired woman in her eighties, with a large nose and olive coloured skin, Nanny Olive was not the sort you could put one over on. She would be ready to put anyone who tried firmly in his or her place. A Londoner through and through, she had a good sense of humour though and could be quite sweet too.

Southwold was a time of chilling out with a couple of other families that they met up with each year. The boys played football on the beach with the other kids and dug huge trenches and holes, with elongated systems of canals to trap the incoming tide. Mum and Dad spent their time reading outside the beach hut, like a pair of old fogeys. Mum swam in the ice-cold water like a true mad woman, with Dad forced to join her on occasions. And all the while, the wind blowing a gale, the waves ducking someone or other under, and the sun shining between the big, white, fluffy clouds. Southwold was a true little old English seaside town. Of course, it wasn't exactly the greatest excitement for a teenage boy like George, but it had its compensations.

There was the Swan Hotel, with its weekday set lunches – slow-cooked leg of duck, delicious terrines for starters, desserts to die for. Their head chef at that time was a genius. George ate in an ecstatic trance, savouring every mouthful, every subtle flavour. The boy loved food; he appreciated food; he would try any food.

There was also the ice cream from the coffee shop – a huge list of flavours and a queue to equal them. There was the fish and chip shop, the bacon sandwiches from Suzie's on the promenade, the pâtés from the deli, an evening stuff-up with sausage, mash and onion gravy at the 'Five Bells'.

George was fifteen – just. He met up with a couple of girls and took to going off for a wander in the early evening. Mum and Dad were pleased for him. The only problem was he fancied the one who didn't fancy him and he didn't fancy the one who did fancy him.

"Oh well, Sod's Law," thought Mum.

But still his jaw tingled, there was a numb patch on his lip and his back teeth felt pressured. Dad took him to a local dentist, who couldn't find anything wrong. And still the tingling and the numbness and the pressure continued. Dad was worrying more and more. It was a cloud developing over them. They returned home at the end of the holiday, none the wiser.

It was the last week of the school holidays when a wisdom tooth suddenly came through at the back of George's mouth. He seemed too young for wisdom teeth and the gum was looking swollen around it. Mum took him to the local dentist, who was definitely concerned. The dentist took an X-ray, which showed that something had grown very fast and pushed the tooth up out of his gum prematurely. She said it was probably just a cyst, but George should be seen by the dental team at St. George's. She wrote a letter in order that they would be able to get an immediate appointment, which she deemed absolutely necessary.

The next day Dad took George to St. George's. Mum stayed at home to pick up Louis, who had been on his Year Five school trip and had passed an exciting few days away on his own for the first time. As she stood amongst the other parents waiting for the coach bringing back the weary travellers, she already had the feeling of being different, separate. Somehow it felt as if her family was in another place now.

At St George's things were not going well, but

there was an urgency to the matter now that caused everything to move very fast. One of the registrars, greatly concerned, called in several other colleagues to examine George and ordered an emergency CT scan. There was a long wait around for the scan result and George, seemingly unconcerned, spent the time playing on his Sony PSP, chatting about inconsequential stuff or just sitting still and bored. It was a pattern of behaviour that he would increasingly adopt over the next couple of years. He and Dad would sit side by side, waiting to be seen by some doctor or other, with George's laid-back posture in contrast to the tense, fidgety figure of his father always fearing the worst.

Once the registrar had looked at the results on the computer, he called the consultants in and Dad and George, observing the clinicians' uncomfortable body language, knew there was something definitely up. Dad, beside himself with worry, couldn't keep still, but George became irritated with him and told him to chill. Then they were seen by surgeons who, fresh up from theatre and still wearing their gowns, confirmed there was a problem on the jaw, which would need to be biopsied the next day. Dad, who knew that only a suspicion of cancer would prompt such urgent action, felt sick. George, however, didn't seem to take in the significance of the urgency. He was busy being impressed by the technology that had created the 3-D image of his skull on the computer screen. He was invited to have a go and he began to swivel the view and zoom in and out of the image. As he zoomed in on the end of the right mandible, just below the ear, they saw that there was a tiny extrusion from the bone and a long, thin root snaking out with a tiny spot on the end of it. Above the exit from the bone was the wisdom tooth, jutting out wildly. Later that evening, Dad spent many hours looking at all the possible things the tumour could be – there were plenty of benign bone growths, and he was desperately hoping it would be one of those.

The next day Mum, Dad and George returned to St George's for the biopsy, after which they came home to wait for the results. Normally there would have been a long wait, but this time there was a phone call from the Marsden the following afternoon, before George arrived home from school. There was bad news; the biopsy result showed that George had a bone cancer – osteosarcoma.

"Is it treatable?" asked Dad.

"Yes, with chemotherapy and surgery," came the reply.

But there was no time to waste. Tests would need to be done, a Hickman Line inserted in his chest, to give drugs or take blood, and chemotherapy started. Chemotherapy might be complicated because of his previous treatment as a child.

"What do I tell George?" asked Dad.

"Tell him it's treatable," said the oncologist.

And so devastation hit. After months of angst and going backwards and forwards between dentists and oncologists, suddenly it was all happening fast. George was now formally diagnosed with a bone cancer – osteosarcoma – of the jaw

Dad had suspected the worst all along, even though the doctors had initially said it was definitely nothing to worry about, as they had when George was little and had developed cancer – when they had said that Dad was just a bit hysterical because his wife had died of cancer and "lightening doesn't strike twice." They were wrong. And now it was striking a third time.

Mum and Dad couldn't understand why it had taken three months to get a diagnosis. Shouldn't the oncologists have known that tingling in the jaw was probably tumour pressing on a nerve, even if it was still too small to see? Mum went on to the Internet and immediately found that tingling in the jaw was usually associated with cancer in the mouth. Shouldn't it have rung some kind of warning bells? Wasn't it about the length of time after radiotherapy that a new cancer could develop? The tumour was, after all, in the exit path of the radioactive beam. The oncologist assured them that the position of the tumour made it unlikely that it had been caused by the radiotherapy George had had as a small child. By now Mum and Dad didn't know what to believe.

They were all in a state of shock, but there were no tears, no strong reactions from George.

He simply asked, "How are you supposed to feel when you've been told you've got cancer?"

He seemed dazed, as if he had never taken the possibility of such a diagnosis seriously. After all, only a few weeks previously he had been told cancer wasn't an issue. But once it was confirmed, he did what any boy his age would do – he went on to the Internet and he found he had a 40% chance of surviving five years. Mum and Dad tried to reassure him, pointing out that statistics could be very misleading. This was an average figure, they said, taking into account all sorts of individuals, who might be further advanced in their cancer, who might be old or very young, or not very healthy. He was not an average; he was his own person, young and healthy; and most importantly, they would fight this all the way. His parents were educated people, who would search out the latest treatments, complementary or mainstream. The Marsden were clearly talking about curing him; they would pull through. And then Mum and Dad had told him about when he was a young boy with cancer and, after two long bouts of chemotherapy, radiotherapy and an operation, there was still evidence of cancer cells remaining. At the time the doctors had told them he had only a five percent chance of survival. This was much worse than the figures he had found and look at him now – still there, a healthy contradiction to their prognosis. Statistics should be taken with a pinch of salt. George seemed to take all this on board and it appeared to help. But who knows what he was feeling inside? They could only imagine.

Dad felt sick inside. His stomach was screwed up into a tight knot. He was terrified, seized by the terrible old fear that he thought had gone away forever – that he would lose his son. He had lost his first wife, nearly lost his son once before and now he was there again. It was an unbearable thought; such a loss would make life unliveable.

Mum feared for him. She was aware that she needed to gather up all her strength to support them through this. They must protect George from the fear of death at all costs. They were agreed on this and they knew they would do everything to get through. And then, of course, there were Louis and Despina to think of.

---o---

When Louis arrived home from school, Mum, Dad and George were all in the sitting room. His parents called him in and asked him to sit down as they wanted to talk to him. He knew then that something was up. They all looked very calm, but serious.

He sat next to his brother on the sofa opposite the fireplace. His mum and dad were sitting on the other one that was set with its back to the bay window. The room was bright with the afternoon sun, the brightness accentuated by the pale yellow painted walls. There were blue patterned curtains and lots of blue covers and striped blue cushions placed on the pale green sofas, and the old Victorian style fireplace had tiles with blue cornflowers on them. Mum would sometimes light a fire on cold winter days. At Christmas they would sit there, in front of a roaring fire, eating turkey sandwiches and watching a film together.

Louis waited in anticipation. Then Dad explained that they had the results of the biopsy and George had cancer again. This time it was a bone cancer in his jaw. Louis was a bit shell-shocked. He turned to his brother.

"Sorry George. Are you ok?"

George replied that he had been better and then

said he was going upstairs.

What did it all mean? Louis knew that people died of cancer, but Mum and Dad said that the hospital were not talking about George dying, they were talking about curing him. This meant that there would be a lot of hospital visits, with overnight stays and they would have to reorganise their lives a bit. They would work out when Mum would go to the hospital and decide what Louis would do. But they wouldn't leave him alone. They were going to make sure George got better, but it was going to take time. Was he ok? They both gave him a hug and said it would be hard, but they were strong and would all get through.

Louis went upstairs and sat on the bed in his little room at the front of the house. The young boy wondered what it all meant. Cancer. He knew it could kill people. It was pretty dramatic. He knew George had had cancer before, but that was something he had heard about in stories from his mum and dad. And of course, George had that dip in the side of his face, where they had removed the muscle with the tumour in it. No one who knew George really took much notice of it; it was just part of George. But it meant he couldn't raise the eyebrow on the left side. He could do what the rest of them couldn't do though – raise just one eyebrow. It was maddening to try to do that and fail, while George just sat there looking questioningly with one eyebrow raised up. He definitely had a knack of turning unfortunate things to his own advantage. But, this?

Mum and Dad had said the hospital was going to

cure George. He hoped they were right. He switched on his computer. He wanted to play a game and forget about it. He heard George playing 'Call of Duty' on his computer in his room at the back. He would leave him alone for a bit. Maybe he'd play with him in a while. He didn't really know what it all meant, but he knew it was bad.

Mum and Dad were still downstairs. They sat on the sofa, exhausted. They held each other close and Dad cried. They chatted quietly for a while, then they pulled themselves together and Mum set about making dinner while Dad began the daunting task of phoning round the family.

---o---

Despina, still at university, was cooking dinner in her little studio flat when Dad rang her. She had only just started her PGCE and was surprised to get a call from him. She was not really aware of the seriousness of the problems George had been having, although she knew his teeth had been playing up since the skin cancer had been removed. When she heard the news, she froze, staring at the sausages sizzling in the frying pan, no idea how to react, except that she heard herself saying, "Ok" and accepting an invitation to come home for the evening. In this strange, removed state she moved into automatic pilot and began to throw her half-cooked dinner in the bin. It was only when she accidentally placed her hand on the scalding hob that she let out a cry, a long scream, so loud and heartfelt that her neighbour came running to her door to check if she was ok.

Dad picked up Despina from the station and on the way to the house he pulled the car over to discuss George's condition. She kept asking him if it was life threatening. What could he say? For the next couple of years he and Mum would have these conversations with family members, attempting to reassure them, to buoy them up, in an attempt to keep everyone afloat, including themselves.

At home, Despina went upstairs to join George and Louis and, when Louis was in bed, Mum and Dad finally sat down together in front of a film to 'veg out'. It had been a long day.

For The Love of George

4. Prodded, Poked, Questioned: Treatment Begins

And so they started a new life.

Dad was clear that they must continue as normally as possible. Mum would carry on with her PhD, Dad would go to work or take his laptop to the hospital, George would carry on at school and take his school work to the hospital, Despina would continue with her PGCE and Louis would go to school. This was the best thing they could do for George. After all, what would he think if they all gave up their jobs? They would live life, not death. Mum was determined they would live, laugh and be full of life, to counteract the gloom.

And George? Somehow he seemed to absorb it all, digest it and move on. He went to school, he met his mates, he attended his many hospital appointments where they explained the chemotherapy protocol he would follow for the next few months. They sent him for scans, cardiograms, kidney function tests – tests for this, tests for that – all of which would continue throughout his treatment. They looked, prodded, poked, questioned, explained and kept him waiting in corridors for many hours. He traipsed those long corridors of the sprawling Royal Marsden Hospital with Mum and Dad by his side, up and down the lifts from one department to another. He had an operation to insert a Hickman Line in his chest, so that he could be given chemotherapy and any other necessary drugs direct into a main artery. And he went to St George's again.

At St George's he met a surgeon called Mr Hyde – a tall, fair-haired man of around fifty with a roundish face. He was a quietly-spoken, pleasant, warm but efficient person, who inspired confidence. Over the months to come he would show the utmost respect for George. He was quite witty in a low-key sort of way and George, Mum and Dad immediately liked him. He shook hands with them and welcomed them into his room and carried out an examination of George's mouth and jaw. He explained that, once the chemotherapy had shrunk the tumour in the jaw sufficiently, he could operate to remove the diseased bone and reconstruct a new half-jaw. He was a maxillofacial surgeon and would be in charge of the whole operation, although there would be other surgeons involved. It would be a major surgical procedure, lasting about twelve hours.

The plan was to reconstruct the new half-jaw with bone taken from elsewhere in George's body, or from a titanium plate (bone from the patient's own body was actually preferable, and was finally opted for by Mr

Hyde, once he had identified that a suitable specimen was available, but titanium screws were used, which later caused a considerable amount of clicking at the jaw joint). Muscle, taken from George's abdomen, would be wrapped around the bone or titanium plate to create some tissue for facial contour and blood vessels would be pulled into the area to connect up to the muscle. The muscle would be large and make George's face look swollen for many months, but it would eventually shrink. There was one possible side effect, Mr Hyde informed them – it would be hard to ensure that there wouldn't be nerve damage, due to the huge amount of fiddly work in the area, including having to pull the main nerve out of the way to carry out the procedure. It could mean that he might develop palsy on the side of his face. Hopefully, it would only be temporary and the nerve would recover and his face return to normal over the following months, but it was not guaranteed. In addition, George would lose all his teeth on the bottom right hand side. This was not good news as it was the side where his bite was better. It was all very daunting.

Mr Hyde asked them to go away and think about whether they wanted to go ahead. George said that he didn't need to do that; he wanted the operation. What real choice was there? He wanted the tumour out as soon as possible. Grinning widely, he began to talk up the positives of having a titanium plate in his jaw and having scars to show off. Mr Hyde said it was typical of the boys. For girls it was harder to rejoice in the prospect of scarring.

After the visit to St George's, Mum and Dad began preparing for the chemotherapy days in the Marsden – four days (three overnight stays) each week for three weeks and then two weeks off to recover, before starting the whole process again. They hoped they would manage to avoid Christmas in hospital. They told friends the news and people commiserated and offered help, including having Louis to stay over so that Mum could go into hospital with Dad and George.

It was funny that Mum had only really begun to be friends with some of the other mums at Louis's school just as he was in his last year there. It was probably because she had been busy with work until recently and hadn't been that connected with the school and the social life that surrounded it. In fact, she had never really wanted to be involved. But she had lost two close female friends to cancer in the last couple of years and felt the loss quite acutely. She was lonely and was pleased when she began to get to know the other mums. It was good to have some women friends locally. And what friends they would turn out to be! They were a continuing source of support and strength, and things would have been a lot worse for Mum, Dad and Louis without them. There were offers to bring round food, fetch shopping, walk the family dog (which they acquired later during George's illness) or simply to have a chat over a cup of coffee. And lovely Natasha, with her calm, motherly ways saved the day by taking care of Louis.

Natasha was Max's mum, who was Louis's best friend. It was decided that Louis would stay the first night of each chemotherapy week at their house. Max had an older brother and sister and the house was often full of young people. There were plenty of screens to play on too, and Max's dad was great with Louis, even referring to him as 'the third son'. Over the months they made Louis feel part of the family and this was worth its weight in gold; it put Mum and Dad's minds at rest. Mum and Dad said they didn't know how they would ever repay them. Little did they know that a few years later that Ian, Max's dad, would be battling with his own cancer.

Louis liked staying at Max's, but was also glad to get back to Mum the next day. While Dad stayed on with George at the Marsden, usually with Despina visiting, Louis and Mum would spend time at home, chilling out and eating dinner in the sitting room, in front of a film. They were special times. On the third evening, they would take dinner into George and Dad and spend time with the two of them and Despina at the hospital, before coming home for the night. That was special too. As the weeks went by, life followed this pattern for Louis – one night at Max's, one night alone with mum, one evening in the hospital with Dad, George and Despina and then back home for the night with mum again. Then Mum would pick up Dad and George from the hospital the next day and bring them home. And so life went on for the family. Treatment proceeded and became a feature of their new life.

At the Marsden, if they were lucky, Mum and Dad would be allocated a room upstairs in the parents' flat, but Dad would always sleep downstairs in the ward with George. Invariably, he and Mum would settle down together on the single fold-out bed next to George, but Mum would often go upstairs for a few hours sleep in the early hours of the morning, unable to even doze, moulded together with Dad into a permanent G for George shape, wedged against the wall and roasting in the unbearable hospital heat.

When George had been in hospital with cancer as a young child, Mum and Dad had slept fine in the single bed in the room George was allocated at Great Ormond Street Hospital. Dad would raid empty rooms and cupboards, to find extra pillows and padded leather cushions, from which they would construct some extra width for the bed, against the wall of the room. They were still fairly supple at that age and would sleep well, despite the intermittent whirring of the chemo drip and the comings and goings of nurses. And for some reason, it wasn't as hot in Great Ormond Street. In the Marsden, George hardly ever had his own room and the disturbances were greater – six chemo machines running in the six-bed wards, nurses coming and going to administer to six patients, children sometimes crying out, adults mumbling – and all the time the unbearable heat.

In the first months of chemo, they managed to commandeer a portable fan for their cubicle. Later on, fans were banned – something to do with health and safety and the circulation of germs. There seemed to be no logic to this. Roasting the patients alive was not considered a health hazard, not to mention the affect of heat on the incubation of germs. But the heating was controlled centrally and the nurses could do little to help. Beds next to the garden door became something of a premium on warm days. If you got one of these, you would be ok, if not you were slow-cooked.

The food wasn't great either, but there was a kitchen on the ward, where food was specially prepared for patients, and the staff tried to be helpful. They would rustle up almost anything George might ask for from the menu, but choice was limited for George, who was trying not to eat too much of the unhealthy food on offer. There was also a small kitchen that parents could utilise and Mum and Dad made use of this. They would bring in home-cooked dishes and reheat them, or make simple meals on the small hob. Upstairs, in the parents' flat, there was a bigger kitchen and, although it was less well equipped, Mum and Dad sometimes used this, when downstairs was too crowded.

On the days when Mum was at home, she would cook and she and Louis would bring in meals, making enough for Dad and George to keep some for the next day. Yiayia and Buppou would also cook for them regularly and in this way, they managed mostly to avoid hospital food. It was ironic that Buppou had been a hospital chef before retirement.

Some of the nurses were great and George, Mum and Dad had particular confidence in one young male nurse who really seemed to know his stuff and was very warm, friendly and efficient. One or two were a bit offish or bossy, but you just got to know not to ask them for anything. Perhaps that's what they wanted. The sisters were cheery, the orderlies were friendly and the registrars who came round were mostly pleasant and efficient.

George slipped into a hospital routine. His nights would invariably be disturbed and, slow to wake from the effects of the chemotherapy drugs, he would often sleep until 9.00 or 10.00 in the mornings. Then he would eat a couple of Weetabix for his breakfast while Mum and Dad tidied up and an orderly cleaned his cubicle. After some nagging from his parents, he would roll out of bed and pay a visit to the bathroom, with chemo pump in tow, to carry out his morning ablutions. A doctor would appear at some point, on morning rounds, to check all was ok. After that, he would reluctantly tackle an hour and a half of schoolwork, before sinking into sleep again, or watching a DVD on his laptop. After lunch, he might be persuaded to focus on his schoolwork again, while Mum took herself off to the parents' flat to concentrate on her PhD work and Dad carried on with his work on his laptop. At around 5 p.m. Yiayia and Buppou would arrive, followed by Despina. Some evenings, aunts and cousins would appear and they would be loud and animated in true Mediterranean style. George would then be persuaded to go to the teenage room, to play a game of table football, greatly enlivened by the competition with his Uncle David – Auntie Ann's husband. Occasionally, during the day, George's two best friends would arrive and they would go off to the teenage room together. He would come alive with his mates, joking and confident in the company of these tall, sociable and protective boys. They would bring him a jokey present – an outlandish tie, a pair of pink gloves, a light-up Christmas headband.

There were good times, even in hospital, but there were also bad days, when George would feel lethargic and low, spending his time dozing on and off, waking only to munch half-heartedly on his lunch or quietly watch a film. Despite this, he knew that he was lucky – unlike many chemotherapy patients – not to suffer from nausea or sickness. This didn't stop the hospital sending him home with a bag full of anti-sickness pills. Mum and Dad tried to hand them back, but to no avail, so they tried instead to stop any more being prescribed. They explained at one point that they had £800 worth of anti-emetic tablets at home that would all end up in the bin, so to speak. But still the pills kept coming and finally they gave up. They began to wonder how much money was wasted in over-prescribed medication and hospital heating.

During George's treatment, Despina started a teaching experience placement in a Sutton school near the Marsden, and therefore she was often able to join Dad and George for dinner. Then, one evening, on her way to catch a bus to the station and return to her bedsit in Guildford, she began looking around at the houses and resolved to move to Sutton, to be closer to George. When she found a new studio flat to rent she was happy to be able to visit George more often. When George was at home, she would come to stay at the house for the weekend and the three siblings would go out together for a meal or to the cinema or just sit on George's bed chilling out in front of a DVD. For the two brothers and their sister, these were good times, with the three of them all together. And when Despina met her boyfriend Tom, who she was later to marry, he would accompany them to the cinema or for a meal. The boys liked the sharp sense of humour of this short, ginger-haired boy. When they all went to the cinema together for the first time and Tom needed to go to the toilet, he commented "Make sure you look out for the ginger glow when I come back in." All through the film George could be heard laughing as he remembered Tom's little joke. George appreciated good humour and he sent Despina a text later that night, saying how funny and cool Tom was.

And so the family slipped into a routine and it became part of their life – living with cancer, not dying from it. Dad began researching, reading piles of medical papers on the latest clinical trials and treatments. Mum had access to electronic versions of medical journals whenever they needed it. Dad had completed his own PhD a couple of years earlier and this stood him in good stead for the task at hand. George, keen to follow any ideas that might help him to survive the disease, began taking a combination of pills and substances alongside the chemotherapy. Dad, who was very thorough and cautious, was always careful to check whether there could be any interference with the chemo drugs. Despite this, they plied George with some horrible substances, some of which did him no good whatsoever.

They also renewed their efforts to feed George healthy food – plenty of fresh fruit and vegetables, not too much meat, wholemeal grain, pulses and fish – plus some homemade treats, like cheesecake on occasions and proper, dark chocolate. It was important to cook good, tasty food, as it was one of George's greatest pleasures. Luckily Mum loved to cook and George was her biggest fan.

Food had been an issue in the family for many years now. When George had had his first cancer Mum and Dad had spent hours enticing him to eat healthy food. It would sometimes take an hour to get him to eat his dinner, with endless games invented to get salad into him. In the end he was by far the least fussy of all the children. Mum and Dad reacted against the advice of the hospital, when he was little, to feed him anything to keep his weight up. Chemotherapy can cause serious loss of appetite and some parents struggled to get even a chocolate bar into their child. In those days, nutritionists would advise high sugar drinks and stodgy white grains – anything to get a child to eat. But Mum and Dad felt this advice was doing a disservice to the children. There were plenty of good, tasty, healthy foods out there, although admittedly it wasn't an easy task to expand and re-educate a child's palate; it required a good deal of time and patience.

Consequently, when George was still only three years old, Mum and Dad became known as the food cranks in the family. They didn't mind though, if it meant they could help to keep their son strong and healthy. They struggled to work against the endless sweetie treats given by people who felt sorry for him and thought he was deprived. They made sure he had at least his 'five a day' and when Louis was born he started life with the same sort of diet. But, as the years passed and George was cancer-free, it grew more difficult to stick to and to convince others, although they never completely gave up the effort. Mum believed good food could really support the body in times of stress. Now, in this new time of stress they needed to return to a stricter regime.

As the first months of treatment passed, George tolerated the chemotherapy reasonably well, without major side-effects. He went to school when he could and studied in hospital when he couldn't. He suffered a good deal of tiredness and experienced some pain in his jaw. In addition, low blood counts lowered his resistance to cold viruses and he spent a couple of short stays in his local hospital with high temperatures and infections. In the early days, a lesion was spotted above his right eyebrow, which caused fears that the tumour had metastasised – that is, spread to other parts of the body. Fortunately, a biopsy showed that the lesion was benign, which was a huge relief, as it meant that the cancer hadn't spread.

Then George's hair fell out. His thick curls lay all over his pillow in the mornings. It was disturbing to see, but not nearly as upsetting as when he had lost his hair as a young child during chemotherapy. Mum remembered the first time she had seen it happen. They had been at Nanny Olive's and Granddad Charlie's – Mum, Dad, George and Despina – sitting round the table having tea, when the first clumps of dark curls had fallen on to the little boy's plate. This time, the teenage George opted to use the clippers and shaved his little remaining hair close, until eventually he became completely bald.

Another disturbing event happened early on in

the treatment – the tumour broke through the jaw and gum into George's mouth. This had probably been caused by the first biopsy (of the jaw), which had involved accessing the tumour through the inside of the mouth. Over the next few weeks it began to sprout into a horrible misshapen grey and white mass of soft tissue at the back of George's mouth, which made it harder for him to eat. One day, after a few weeks of treatment, he was admitted to his local hospital with a high temperature. It was a short stay, but Mum and Dad would never forget it. George, poorly with a virus of some kind, was barely able to swallow because of the size of the soft tissue tumour now growing towards the back of his throat. They were terrified his throat would close up. Luckily it didn't.

Eventually, the chemotherapy began to work on the soft tissue and bits of it started to break off. George became an expert at rinsing and spitting, making sure he didn't swallow any of it. It was a relief to see the horrible mass inside his mouth diminishing rapidly. However, it was a different story with his jawbone, which was still swollen and reducing only very slowly. As they moved towards Christmas, Mum and Dad began to wonder how successful the chemotherapy was going to be.

For The Love of George

5. "Only me, then"

The question had been raised as to why George had suffered from three different cancers in his short life. In order to attempt to answer this question, the family were referred to the Institute of Cancer Research (ICR) for genetic testing; it was possible that George had a gene defect.

On a cold, windy morning in November 2008 George, Mum and Dad set off to meet with a petite, Asian woman at the ICR, who was a professor of human genetics. The ICR buildings were situated in extensive grounds behind the Royal Marsden Hospital in Sutton. On arrival, they were met on the ground floor of the modern, glass building by the professor's PA and escorted up to a small office on the first floor, passing flowing palms and a bustling little café on the way. By now, George was used to the many interruptions to his schooling; it was becoming the new 'norm' for him. And of course he had grown up with regular hospital visits and examinations by various doctors.

The professor, like Mr Hyde, was efficient, yet

warm and very thorough in explaining the range of disorders that might have affected George, including a rare one called Li Fraumeni Syndrome – the most likely one indicated by his profile. She was a sympathetic person, but did not underplay the potential seriousness. At the end of the meeting, George, not one to procrastinate, opted to have the test – a simple blood test – and the family went home to await the results, which would take a few weeks to process.

If George tested positive there were implications for other members of the family; the disorder was hereditary. The ensuing wait was difficult. Mum and Dad, meanwhile, decided not to inform anyone outside the immediate family, as there seemed no point in increasing everyone else's anxiety levels.

When the test results came back some weeks later it transpired that George did have Li Fraumeni Syndrome (LFS), something they had not heard of before meeting the professor. They learnt that this was one of the most serious of the cancer predisposition syndromes as it involves a mutation of the TP53 gene. This gene is known to function as a tumour suppressor by creating the p53 protein, itself central to the mechanism that kills cells that become malignant. It meant that George's body was missing one of the key processes for stopping damaged cells from forming cancers[1]. For many people who

---

[1] Later, Dad would formulate and publish a new theory about LFS and its relationship with the metabolism and premature ageing of cells, predisposing sufferers to develop cancer (see Li Fraumeni Syndrome, Cancer and Senescence: A New Hypothesis, Pantziarka, P., *Cancer Cell International* 2013, 13:35)

develop cancer, the TP53 gene becomes damaged only in their tumours, but it functions normally in the rest of the body. For someone with LFS it is a different story – a permanent state throughout the whole body. Born with a damaged TP53 gene, the risk of getting cancer was incredibly high for George. If he survived his current cancer he could develop a new one at any time. It was not a foregone conclusion that this would happen, but there was a high chance of it. And, to make things worse, there was very little research being undertaken into this rare syndrome. There were no support groups, no charities, no central information resources in the UK and many doctors, including oncologists, knew little or nothing about LFS. As they had feared, it also meant that other people in the family could be affected; it was hereditary. The news was shocking.

Dad took the test; he was clear. The implications therefore were that the problem had either started with George – which was possible – or that it had been passed down from his natural mother, who had died of ovarian cancer at the very young age of 29. Louis, at least, would be unaffected, as he had a different mother. Despina, however, might not.

It was a tense time while Despina went to pre-test counselling, took the test and waited to discover whether she was affected or not. Fortunately, some weeks later, she learnt that she was also free of the disorder.

"Only me, then," said George.

It was a relief, but also terribly unfair. Only George, then. Mum and Dad wondered how they were to protect him in the future. Dad now had a new area to research, but for the present they had to focus on getting him through his current cancer.

Mum and Dad made the difficult decision not to tell the rest of the family just yet. It would be hard keeping this terrible knowledge to themselves, especially for George, but they had no desire to cause more stress amongst family members. When other family members were stressed it was also more difficult for Mum and Dad to cope. And so they lived with the knowledge, keeping up appearances and secretly worrying. This is how they would live for the next couple of years. They would always keep something back, from George, from Louis, from Despina, from everyone because they could neither risk frightening George, nor did they want to overload others; they needed those around them to stay strong. Sometimes the strain of it was unbearable, but they did it to try and hold everyone together. And they had each other. Without each other they were nothing. Not that other family members were not supportive; the family rallied round to help and did what they could. But day-to-day the burden was heavy and without each other's support Mum and Dad would both have sunk, along with George.

Meanwhile, the treatment for osteosarcoma continued, but the tumour in the bone was resilient and by Christmas it had shrunk only a small amount. Despite this, Mr Hyde said he was prepared to operate, which the family was glad to hear as George, Mum and Dad were keen to have the tumour removed as soon as possible. But their oncologist wanted to give more chemotherapy to try and further shrink the tumour. George had now had the maximum dose of one of the drugs in the first chemo protocol, and therefore would need to switch to a second-line protocol, which wasn't considered to be as widely effective. George was not happy; Mum and Dad were not happy. Mr Hyde had said he was willing to operate, but would be guided by their oncologist at the Marsden. And so they bowed to her superior knowledge. Later they regretted it.

Alison, their oncologist at the Marsden, was a tall, fair-haired, middle-aged, female consultant, who was also a professor and was held in high esteem. She had a serious, focused manner, was articulate and did not 'beat around the bush'. Mum and Dad sometimes felt her approach was rather negative and, as time went by, they found themselves in disagreement with more than one of her decisions. However, she seemed to be a woman of some integrity who came to see George when he was treated in other hospitals, gave her email address and mobile number to Dad and seemed to take a genuine interest in George's well-being. For the moment, her word was final.

---o---

Christmas arrived. They had an appointment with Alison at the Marsden on Christmas Eve, but they were home by the evening and George would be at home for the whole Christmas period!

Preparations for Christmas were already underway. Mum and Louis had put up the Christmas tree earlier that week and they were busy cooking. There were certain Christmas rituals that had to be observed. First of all, the tree had to be real. Mum would get down the big box of old traditional decorations and she and the children would unwrap them and lay them out on a tray in the sitting room, before hanging them on the tree. Their tree never looked anything like those you saw in the shops, all beautifully colour-coordinated, but Louis thought theirs was better. Mum tried to explain to Dad that a real tree looked and smelled good, but Dad didn't really get it, the old curmudgeon. Usually, he would curse and complain about how awkward it was to get it set up and would finally end up upsetting Mum, who then wouldn't speak to him for a good couple of hours, while the boys sighed at the sight of two grown people squabbling and sulking over a tree. This year Mum took it upon herself to sort it out using her own system, with – as she smugly pointed out – very little bother.

Mum always went mad on the cooking at Christmas. She made her own Christmas puddings, Christmas cake etc. Louis would spend hours assisting her on Christmas Eve, making the mince pies, sausage rolls and stuffing. In years past, both he and George had been the mince pie helpers and there were photos of them hard at work in the kitchen. With George being a teenager now, preferring to eat rather than cook, Louis was the sous chef. And at this stage in his growing up, that's exactly what he wanted to become – a chef. Sometimes he would chat to Mum about his plans for his own restaurant down by the sea or the river, with the car he would own parked outside.

This year they made vanilla panacotta, to be served with cherries in amaretto syrup, a dark chocolate log with fresh cream filling and a raisin and Armagnac cake. They made pork balls stuffed with apricots and almonds and, on Christmas morning, they rolled the bacon round the chipolatas to roast with the turkey (which Dad had a habit of cooking upside down). Mum made lovely gravy from the turkey juices and Dad made cranberry sauce. George, who was always impressed by the sheer size of the turkey, approved of the large quantities of meat being prepared.

In the midst of all the preparations for the family, Mum and Louis made mince pies for the two middle-aged sisters who lived next door. In return the family always received a huge crate of satsumas, scattered with chocolate coins and other goodies and everyone loved having the huge pile to dip into whenever they wanted.

On Christmas Eve, Despina came home and did her usual job of arranging all the presents under the tree. And on Christmas day, just before dinner, they all sat in the sitting room with a glass of champagne. They went round and took it in turns to say what they wanted to achieve in the next year. Of course, everyone said that they wanted to see George well again. This Christmas they were all optimistic. George's tumour had begun shrinking slowly and, although the operation had been put off till March, he would have more chemo after Christmas and hopefully he would be fine before the end of the school year. George said that he wanted the tumour out, his GCSEs over and to move on to a new place to do his 'A' levels. In the next academic year, he would start a new life, with plenty of socialising. He came as close as he ever would to articulating his desperate need to be over the hurdle that was putting his life on hold. Despina was going to finish her PGCE and get a job teaching; Mum wanted to finish her PhD thesis – or at least the first draft – by the end of the year; Louis wanted to expand his cooking skills to be able to cook something by himself. And Dad? He could only think of getting George well.

Christmas then continued in much the usual fashion, with a blow-out on food, eventual rest on Boxing Day for Mum and Dad and the usual family rows. A few days after Christmas, Mum, Dad and the boys headed up to Southwold for a second Christmas with Nanny Olive.

Mum loved this part of the Christmas holidays more than any other – bracing walks along the beach, gambling two pences in Southwold's only amusement arcade and playing the crazy machines on the pier, invented by the newspaper cartoonist, Tim Hunkin – like the one where you had to hold your hand inside a cage containing the head of an evil-looking German Shepherd, its slavering mouth open wide and full of sharp teeth. Suddenly the dog would bark loudly and you were rated on how quickly you chickened out and yanked your hand out. In addition, there was the meal at 'The Swan' and their own New Year's Day lunch at the place they were staying in, with the traditional champagne toast.

In the winter, they always stayed in a ground floor flat overlooking the sea. From the sitting room with the large bay window they could watch the world go by, while lazing on big squidgy sofas. And behind the sitting room, separated by glass doors, was a large, well-equipped kitchen, where they would bring Nanny Olive for a roast chicken dinner.

Mum and Louis would invariably do some mad walk in the freezing cold, in the wind and rain or snow, down to the harbour and then back through the fields, or something like that. They would stuff bits of tissue in their ears, as well as wearing hats, to keep out the biting cold wind, and they would arrive back soaked through and shivering. George, who was singularly unimpressed by their madness, was not about to put himself through such an ordeal or make such an idiot of himself and so he and Dad stayed in the warmth of the flat, reading their books, happy in father and son companionship.

But soon, after a few days of rest, and having seen in the New Year, it was time to return home to the reality of treatment.

For The Love of George

6. The Waiting Game

By early January they were back into hospital routine with a new chemotherapy protocol in progress. It felt like a long haul, but they were optimistic still. George was helped through by constant texting from a young woman he had met in Southwold. Apparently she wasn't one of the two girls from the summer holiday and Mum and Dad couldn't work out just when or how he had met her, but George was giving nothing away. He spent every day sending and receiving texts and calls, to the point where his mobile phone bill gave considerable cause for alarm. He also had plenty of schoolwork to occupy him, as he would be taking his GCSEs in May. He had decided to drop some subjects because it just wasn't realistic to try and take all nine GCSEs while undergoing treatment. There was a schoolroom at the Marsden, run by a very helpful lady, but George wasn't keen on going there and preferred to get help from Mum and Dad. They nagged him constantly to do a certain amount of work each day, even when he was struggling to wake up from the effects of the chemo. Sometimes he voiced his displeasure in no uncertain terms and his parents were forced to back off.

Mum and Dad always pushed George hard. They didn't want him to become a victim, to lose out on opportunities. Most of all, they wanted him to be looking to a future. Perhaps they should have eased off a bit, but despite his protests at times, George knuckled down as best he could under the circumstances – chemo, hospital appointments, scans, more prodding and poking, school, revision, exhaustion; there was no let-up.

Of course there were relaxing interludes – a weekend with the cousins, or a weekend spent with his sister. George and Louis and Despina crammed into her bedsit, eating roast chicken, watching films or wandering round the town of Guildford (before she moved to Sutton). One day in the school holidays, George visited her and she showed him around the university where she had studied for her degree – the campus, the halls of residence, the favourite drinking venues. He thought it was the coolest thing.

Then Mum had an idea. George had always wanted a dog. The parents had always said no because they were away one weekend in four visiting Nanny Olive, plus Mum and Dad had both been out at work before. It was possible that Mum would go back to work after completing her PhD, but she began to think perhaps they could cross that bridge when they came to it. It would be something special for George to look forward to, to get him through the chemo and the operation.

First of all they needed to check it out with Louis, who was, unfortunately, terrified of dogs. Would he be able to handle the idea? And they would need to tell Despina, who wasn't fond of animals and had also been afraid of dogs when she was younger. In fact, even George had suffered from this fear as a young child. What a family! Mum blamed Dad.

Louis said he would do it somehow for George. Despina said she would never come to the house again if they got a dog, but they took this with a pinch of salt. She had once threatened to kill her flatmate's rabbit, but somehow it lived to a grand old age and they knew she would come round for George's sake.

Telling George about the dog was great; he was just stunned. At first he didn't believe it. And he was so excited. Mum and Dad said they should wait until he had finished his chemo and the operation was over, before actually getting the dog. But it gave George something good to focus on and from that moment he spent hours every week looking at dogs for sale on the Internet.

Through January and February the weeks passed slowly. The tumour was only reducing very slightly and the wait for the operation was dragging on. But in February there was a pleasant break from routine, when they were snowed in. Schools were closed; Dad couldn't get to work. George was full of energy compared to recent weeks and enjoyed having a couple of days to chill out at home, free from hospital appointments and school. The roads were thick with snow, the garden was knee deep in the stuff and Louis wanted to make a snowman.

And so, Mum and Louis trudged into the back garden mid-morning, the snow crunching under their wellies, while Dad was working at his computer and George was doing some teenage 'chillaxing' in his room. The garden had been transformed into an unknown landscape – a collection of white mounds, with the trees, now a canopy of white, reflecting the low winter sun. Doing their best to avoid where they took the flowerbeds to be in the tightly-packed little garden, Mum and Louis set to work.

After a period of hard graft the snowman began to take shape and Mum's back began to complain, but they laboured on until they had the basic shape, encouraged by a cup of coffee and biscuits supplied by Dad. The end result, an hour or so later, was a fine snowman, with coal for the eyes, a black pipe cleaner mouth, the obligatory carrot for a nose and more coal as buttons. They commandeered Dad's old black scarf and George, who had come to have a look, donated a blue-and-white-striped, woollen hat with a peak. Photos were taken and congratulations were forthcoming.

The snowman lasted for a few days before finally melting away into that little sad heap of snow where all snowmen meet their end. Later in the year the photos were transformed into Christmas cards by Louis and Mum. She loved these traditional rituals. She regarded them as very important to family life, a way of providing stability and giving children memories on which to build a future. They formed a basis for family traditions to be passed down the generations. Family rituals and celebrations were also her way of giving to her stepchildren, when she fell down on other aspects of what a parent should give, when the day-to-day love or nurturing was not all it should have been.

After a couple of days everyone was back to work or school. The snow was gone, the dream-world of white, when normal daily life pauses for a moment, was past. The world was a busy place again and the noise of rush-hour traffic returned to the bedroom in the mornings. Chemo was delayed for a day, while the hospital caught up with the backlog caused by the bad weather, but on Wednesday they were back in the Marsden and Louis was staying at Max's. George joined Facebook and there began a long relationship of conversations with his mates and old friends, which helped to keep him in touch with that side of his identity when he was in hospital or at home recovering from treatment. He kept friends informed of his progress, with a certain amount of humour and bravado.

Following a scan involving an injection of radioactive dye, he posted – "im banned from goin school tmrw cos i'll be radioactive (smiley face)"

In the end the second protocol of chemo barely reduced George's tumour at all. In fact, in March the tumour had begun to break through into his mouth once more. Mum and Dad were terrified it would grow into his throat again. The wait for the operation seemed endless.

George posted on Facebook, referring to himself in the third person (as he was to do so often with his Facebook postings) "is a proffesional at having cancer."

This was followed shortly by "has been given the 30th march as his operation date nd is gettin a tiny bit shook." At last the date had been set.

Meanwhile, Alison at the Marsden referred them to a doctor at Great Ormond St Hospital, who was leading a cancer vaccine trial that George would be eligible to sign up for after his operation. If the vaccine worked it would be a safeguard against the tumour coming back, or against any micro-metastases (which might be lurking in George's body) taking off and growing.

George, Mum and Dad went to Great Ormond St in central London to meet the man in charge. George was not too keen on signing up for the trial because it involved having injections and he hated injections. Ever since he was tiny he had been afraid of them. He would tolerate all sorts of invasive treatments, but go into hysteria over an injection. When he was younger, just the sight of the needle would be enough to set him off. Everyone has his bottom line.

One day, when he was about nine years old and still attending the follow-up clinic at the Marsden, he was nervously awaiting the insertion of a cannula into his hand so that a dye could be injected into his veins prior to an MRI scan. He was already working himself into a state and the waiting was making things worse. Mum and Dad kept urging him to look away when the needle went in, assuring him that he wouldn't feel any pain as he had had an anaesthetic cream applied to the back of his hand. But George, stubborn as ever, would always look directly at the needle puncturing his skin. This time the procedure was to be carried out by a doctor, who finally arrived, and the wire trolley containing the needles and wipes etc was in position next to George. The doctor fumbled around for a while, but was at last ready to begin and picked up the needle. George, sitting on Dad's lap, with Mum kneeling down in front of him, tensed like an iron rod. The doctor moved toward George, but unfortunately somehow managed to catch the trolley with his elbow, sending it flying and at the same time scattering needles, sachets and dressings everywhere. Then, instead of leaving it for a nurse to clear up, the doctor turned away from George, put the needle down and began scrabbling around on the floor to pick everything up. By the time he returned to his patient, seemingly oblivious to George's distress, the boy was shaking and crying loudly and had to be held and forced to sit still by Dad – all for what should have been a twenty second procedure. And it often was of course – especially when it was performed by nurses.

So, with a history of fearing injections – despite the fact that he must have had well over a hundred in his lifetime – George was not looking forward to the possibility of being subjected to a whole series of vaccinations.

Enrolment in the trial required a sample of live tumour to be taken in order to develop a vaccine that would be personal to the patient. It meant attending the hospital frequently for some months and George would probably be subject to a raised temperature and flu-like symptoms, at least in the early stages. He was worried that this would interfere with the new social life he was planning when he changed schools. He was now very focused on starting a new cancer-free life once the tumour was removed and looking forward to plenty of social activity to compensate for the rough year he was having. Mum and Dad, however, were keen that George should sign up for the trial and they set about unashamedly trying to convince him. Eventually he agreed, if somewhat reluctantly.

In order to facilitate the live tumour sample being available, Dad spoke to Mr Hyde at St George's and to the pathology department there. He impressed on the pathologists the need for a post-operative, 'live' sample and he arranged for it to be urgently transported to Great Ormond Street in the appropriately marked container supplied by the latter. In addition, the consultant leading the trial made a formal request for the sample. Dad was eventually satisfied that he had covered all angles. Unfortunately, later on he was to realise that this was not the case.

Meanwhile the wait for the operation dragged on. 22nd March 2010: George posted on Facebook – "wants this week to go quiiiiiicck."

So did they all.

7. The First Operation

Eventually the day they had all been waiting for arrived. One Sunday lunchtime – 29th March 2010 – Mum, Dad, George, Louis and Despina sat round the dining room table. George's operation was scheduled for Monday morning and they planned to set off for St George's mid-afternoon on the Sunday.

Mum had made roast chicken – George's favourite – and a blueberry cheesecake for dessert. It was a tense time, full of anticipation, as they sat eating their lunch together, but they were all glad the day was at last here. They tucked into the chicken and then ate two thirds of the cheesecake, saving the rest to take with them to the hospital as a treat for later. Then they quickly cleared up, collected their bags and piled into the car. Unfortunately the family Zafira had chosen this particular weekend to break down and would be 'out of service' for a week, but at least they had a replacement car for Mum to drive back and forth to the hospital. And so, after dropping Louis off at Max's, where he was to stay for a couple of nights, they drove on to St George's.

As they passed the familiar shops and schools en route, turning briefly on to the busy A3 before picking up the long road that led to Tooting High Street, Dad sat rigidly in the passenger seat, speaking only to give Mum directions. He was a bundle of nerves. There were so many fears – that the operation would be cancelled for some reason or that it would go wrong in some way; that the procedure would fail to leave a margin clear of disease. And he was afraid of how hard it would be for George. Scared, scared, scared; so much fear. But there was also a desperate hope that somehow it would all turn out well – that George would be George and he'd cope with it all, that it wouldn't be too disfiguring and that it would get rid of the disease once and for all. There was always hope, always a goal to hold in one's mind, keeping the fear under control – just.

At the hospital George was settled into a small, six-bedded room in the children's ward, a few floors up in one of the taller hospital buildings. Yiayia and Buppou were there, but after they left along with Despina, a small crowd of George's school friends arrived to distract him and keep him company. The boys went off to explore, with George in good form, bantering with his friends as they left the ward. Mum and Dad went for a cup of tea and a wander, pleased that George's friends had turned out for him. It was good to see him being just a normal kid with his mates.

When Mum and Dad returned to the ward, the boys were settled on and around George's bed, watching TV, texting on their phones and occasionally making short comments to each other about the programme they were watching. When evening came, the friends left and Mum, Dad and George were finally alone. They ate the food they had brought from home and tried to amuse themselves as best they could – George watching TV, Mum and Dad reading.

George posted on Facebook "is in hospital, bring on tmrw!!"

The hours were passing slowly, but finally, when it was time to sleep, Mum and Dad as so often before settled down beside George on a single pull-out bed. Would any of them sleep?

---o---

The next morning the air was full of unspoken tension. The surgeon and his team visited, followed by one of the anaesthetists who would be involved. George, of course, wasn't allowed to eat; Dad felt sick and couldn't eat; Mum was hungry as usual, but just wanted things to get moving – they all did. George was as uncomplaining as ever and waited quietly for the whole business to get started.

George would be 'under' for about twelve hours and there would be several doctors involved in the procedure. One surgeon would be in charge of taking muscle from his abdomen and replacing it with wire gauze. This was the muscle that would be used to wrap around the newly constructed half jaw. Almost the whole of the right side of the jaw would be removed by Mr Hyde and his team, with George's hip providing bone for the replacement. This latter would be shaped, positioned, the muscle wrapped around it, blood vessels connected and everything sewn back up – a masterpiece of engineering in the body. On the one hand it appeared to be a case of extreme butchery; on the other, a delicate, fiddly, creative and demanding task, involving the utmost skill and patience, not to mention extremely honed fine motor skills.

Dad held on to George's hand all the way down to the operating theatre. George handled himself well, keeping his nervousness under control and making no fuss whatsoever. In the pre-op room Mum and Dad were allowed to stay with George, who was on top form, making little quips to the anaesthetists as they prepared the lines and the drugs. He asked if they had any gas and air, as Dad had said it was good when Mum was giving birth to Louis. Finally, he was given the drug that would send him under; Mum and Dad cried.

The moment of going under, seeing your child so helpless, slipping away into an unknown sleep, is a difficult one. Mum and Dad cried every time. Out in the stark, hospital corridor they were comforted by the nurse and then by the same registrar – part of Mr Hyde's team – who had ordered the revealing CT scan months before. The registrar said something that in the haze of the moment they took little note of, but in the months to come his words would return to haunt them. He assured them that George was in the best hands, that he was having the optimum treatment for his disease, that the only truly effective treatment for osteosarcoma of the jaw was removal by surgery. This, he explained, was because the disease in the jaw, unlike in the long bones of the arms and legs, did not respond well to other treatments such as chemotherapy.

Weeks later they would remember these words and wonder why George had not had the operation sooner, when the surgeon had been prepared to go ahead? Why risk trying a less effective chemotherapy protocol, when the first protocol had showed only minimal success, if surgery was the only truly effective treatment? Why, why, why? For the present, they were ignorant of these questions that would return to torture them many times. For the present they were concerned only for George under the surgeon's knife.

They went for a cup of tea in one of the big hospital canteens. St George's was a huge hospital – a conglomeration of smaller hospitals all now united into one enormous institution. It comprised a set of sprawling concrete blocks – both high and low rise – long windowless corridors, big steel lifts, a medical school, several small cafés and a couple of large canteens. It was grey, busy and unattractive.

Mum and Dad felt empty. They were becoming aware of the long day that lay ahead. They drank their tea, ate their toast and left for the accommodation block where they would later spend the night while George was in intensive care. The room was on the seventh floor and it was bare apart from two single beds, a couple of shelves, a chair and a small sink. The starkness was accentuated by the single light glaring from its old-fashioned yellow shade, hanging down from the centre of the ceiling. Later in the week, Mum would be given a better room, followed by an even nicer one in the swish, new parents' accommodation block, which was funded and run by a charity. But for now they were installed in this suitably depressing high-rise abode. They pushed the beds together and lay down on top of them. Curled up in each other's arms, they fell asleep, partly from exhaustion and partly from the need to pass time.

Fifteen minutes later Dad's mobile went off and the calls from the family began, enquiring how everything was going. They dozed in this disturbed way for a couple of hours. When they woke it was noon and there were at least nine hours to go before they would hear anything. They decided to get up and, given that the nurses had Dad's mobile number, seek out some lunch off-site.

Not far from the hospital entrance, situated along busy Tooting High St, they found an Indian restaurant. It was pretty empty, but looked ok and here they ate a light lunch of Southern Indian cuisine. They chatted about nothing of much consequence, as they dipped their stuffed pancakes into the traditional sambar and scooped up the coconut chutney; it was hard to get the energy to talk. Then they took a walk around the hospital grounds, which wasn't very inspiring. Afterwards, they returned to their room on the seventh floor and read for a while.

They had decided that the time had come to tell the family about George's TP53 gene; it wasn't fair to burden George with keeping it quiet any longer and everyone was going to need to know at some point. It would be easier to deal with this task while George was asleep, when he would not have to cope with other people's grief on top of everything else. Dad had already told his sister – Auntie Ann – in preparation. She would pass it on to other members of the family, except for Yiayia and Buppou; Auntie Ann was going to bring Buppou – who was finding the endless hours of waiting at home unbearable – to the hospital to meet Mum and Dad. It would be a good opportunity to break the news.

When Auntie Ann and Buppou arrived, they all bought tea to take away and sat in a glassed-in seating area near one of the entrances; they wanted somewhere quiet to talk. Thankfully, it was fairly empty and they sat at a little table nursing their plastic cups. Dad broke the news; Buppou cried. It was so hard for him and Yiayia to think of their grandson, who had been through so much already in his short life, suffering even more. He had lost his mother when he was a baby, suffered cancer as a small child and was now undergoing a twelve-hour operation, which could leave him permanently disfigured. They had looked after him as a baby, Yiayia taking the place of his mother and forming a bond that was as close as any mother/child relationship. It was as if the life of one of their own children was threatened. Buppou was distraught.

Mum and Dad left it to Buppou and Auntie Ann to break the news to Yiayia; they knew she would find it even harder to cope with. It was likely to involve a lot of crying and physical distress and the hospital was no place to tackle it. They told Buppou not to wait for George to wake up, as it would be very late and probably they would only be allowed a brief visit; he was going to be kept asleep until the next morning anyway. And sometimes, Mum and Dad just needed to be alone with each other in order to cope.

The rest of the day passed in a pedestrian way, apart from checking into the ward a couple of times to see if there was any news, but all they heard was that everything was going according to plan. At least that was some relief.

By eight o'clock in the evening they were getting edgy. It was hard to occupy themselves any more as the time drew nearer. Finally they decided to take a walk up to the ward to see if there was any news. The nurses rang down to theatre; all was fine, but it would be another hour maybe before George was out of theatre. After receiving assurance that someone would be in touch as soon as there were any further developments, Mum and Dad went back to the room for a while. When they returned to the ward once more, they were informed it would be another half-hour and again they returned to the room.

At last, at 10 p.m. they received a call; George was out of theatre, in the recovery room and doing fine. They should give it half an hour by which time he would be in Intensive Care, where they could visit him briefly. There was just time to make hurried phone calls to family and friends before making their way across the dimly-lit hospital grounds, back through the long corridor of the medical school and up the lift to the intensive care unit.

They knew there would be swelling; they had been warned. And the swelling would be even worse the next day – partly from the surgery itself and partly from the size of the muscle wrapped around the bone. The former would go down before the muscle would shrink, which would take several months. They were also aware that the first 24 hours were crucial because the newly-connected blood vessels, feeding the muscle flap around the bone, could stop pumping, thereby causing the muscle to die. They wouldn't be out of the woods for a week, but the first twenty-four hours were critical.

All the way up to the intensive care unit, Mum kept trying to picture how George would look, trying to prepare herself for something she had no experience of. She held tight on to Dad's hand. By the time they reached the ward, Dad was beside himself with desperation to see George. They rang the bell, washed their hands at the alcohol dispenser in the corridor and a nurse came to the door and asked them to wait in the waiting room. Dad paced, until Mr Hyde appeared, looking tired but confident. He explained that all had gone according to plan; it had just taken a long time. He reiterated that the first 24 hours were critical, and explained that George would be kept sedated until the surgical team visited in the morning, around 8.00. After he left, Mum and Dad were shown on to the ward.

As they entered the extremely clinical atmosphere of Intensive Care, they scanned the extent of the room for a sight of George. They spotted him in a side cubicle to the right of the door, separated from the main ward by a glass partition and surrounded by machines monitoring his pulse, his breathing and his oxygen levels.

There were innumerable lines coming out of his lean, young body, or attached to his chest with pads, and connected up to the machines or drip pumps. As Mum and Dad entered, a young nurse sitting at a small table at the foot of the bed greeted them quietly. She had in front of her a huge chart and was studying on the monitor the digital lines that were rising and falling sometimes rhythmically, sometimes more erratically. She also glanced from time to time at the pulsing numbers on the machines behind and to the side of George and made notes on the chart, all the while keeping a weather eye on the patient.

The swelling was impressive by any standards and it was already beginning to turn black and blue. Dad rushed to George's side and placed his hand on his son's. The nurse offered them chairs and Dad sat, speaking softly to George, saying Mum and Dad were here and that he was ok and they would be there when he woke in the morning. They stayed a little while like that, with both of them stroking his head and chatting quietly to him and then they left. They went to bed in the stark room in the accommodation block and slipped into the sleep of the exhausted, yet not relaxed.

---o---

At 7.00 the next morning Dad was up and by 7.40 he and Mum were once again ringing the bell of Intensive Care, but were somewhat disconcerted to learn that George was already awake. He had woken some time earlier and been allowed to stay conscious. Mum and Dad were upset that they hadn't been there, but George, although looking swollen and weak, was ok about it. After all, as far as he was concerned the most important thing was that the tumour was out of him. At that point he was more concerned about getting the oxygen tube out of his throat; it was extremely uncomfortable and rendered him more helpless in that it prevented him from talking.

In order to communicate, everything had to be written on a notepad, which was difficult as he could barely move his head to see what his hands were writing on the pad he was somehow balancing on his chest. More than once, Mum and Dad had to ask him to repeat something. But the oxygen tube would only be removed when it was certain that George's airway was clear and he was properly awake and able to breathe easily. There were still lines coming out of him all over – for draining the wound in the abdomen, the wound in the hip, the wound in the neck; lines for monitoring this and that; a catheter. Mum and Dad counted 14 in all, including the monitor lines, but within hours several of these had been removed. The first was the oxygen tube, which turned out to be singularly unpleasant, as it made George retch badly and he was sick. However, once it was out, he could talk and he had taken the first of many steps towards recovery.

And this is how they went on. Each time a line came out, each time he achieved something new – getting out of bed, sitting in a chair, walking to the toilet – they celebrated one step nearer to leaving the hospital, to recovery.

By the first afternoon after the operation George was back on the ward – another step forward. He hadn't liked it in Intensive Care, with all the machines, the ultra-clinical setting, the endless to-ings and fro-ings and the distress of other equally helpless patients. He was relieved to get back on the children's ward.

He posted on Facebook "feels pretty shit."

Meanwhile, Mum went home mid-morning and returned with Louis late in the afternoon. They were planning to both stay the night in the accommodation block, while Dad slept on the ward with George, as he would do for the rest of their two-week stay.

When Mum and Louis arrived in the afternoon, George's bed was surrounded by visitors – there was Auntie Ann, Uncle David, his two older female cousins, and Yiayia and Buppou, plus Dad and Despina. George was nervous about his lines and constantly in discomfort, but he appreciated the visitors. He took it all in his stride; he was used to being the centre of attention in the family. There were cards and presents everywhere – an Yves St Laurent shirt from Auntie Ann, flowers, fruit, car and computer magazines.

Underneath all this surface activity George was dealing with things. The drain from the hip was causing problems. It seemed that the nurses on the children's ward were not used to handling post-operative patients of this level of need and complexity. The drain had to be emptied frequently or it caused pressure, with fluid backing up into the wound – an unpleasant enough sensation, but also extremely unnerving. Some of the nurses found the drain difficult to handle. One nurse even asked George how the doctors did it, which didn't inspire confidence. George began to panic. Several times, over the next week, the doctors would have to be called to advise on these little problems – little by comparison to the scale of the operation and the context of a life-threatening disease, but to George they were frightening. What if the drain backed up so much that the wound opened? What if it came out? What if something terrible happened and the doctors couldn't come immediately? What if the nurses didn't know what to do? His friends, sister and cousins were ever supportive through Facebook. They addressed him as 'Babe' and 'Darling', especially the boys, who adopted a jokey, matey approach, which did not detract from their obvious concern. George was clearly genuinely grateful for their concern.

On 3rd April he posted "thanks everybody supportin him through this (smiley face) xxx."

To add to his distress, George was moved into a six-bedded room where the other occupants were all infants or babies. One baby screamed constantly. His Facebook post was not complementary.

"has a complete tard of a nurse lookin after him tnite, wont be gettin much sleep then lol."

After a few days of this, George was becoming depressed. The only times he perked up was when Mr Hyde and his team visited. They were efficient, reassuring and pleased with his progress, which gave him some confidence, but by the end of the first week things were so bad that Auntie Ann began to make some enquiries. She worked in a hospital as a consultant's PA and fortunately knew her way around the system. She made contact with the manager of the children's ward, explained George's situation to her and asked that he be moved to a more appropriate setting. The manager called Mum and Dad in for a meeting. She commented that post-operative patients often experienced depression, but she understood the huge pressure George was under and agreed that he should be relocated. This was finally done in the second week – good old Auntie Ann! There was great relief all round, to see George begin to return to his usual self despite being 'nil by mouth' for over a week, fed gunk through a feeding tube and deprived of gourmet delights, as well as having his speech affected by the surgery.

His Facebook post read "thinks lithpths are cool (now that he has one)."

As George experienced more and more hospital treatment over the following year or so, Mum and Dad came to know when he was on the mend because he would become decidedly stroppy. He would order his dad around, berate him for his inefficiency at executing simple tasks, grunt in reply to questions and generally display an aura of displeasure. At first it was hard to take, but later on they came to understand this was part of the healing process – the frustration at not being able to move or eat properly, the prospect of several more days stuck in hospital when he was beginning to feel stronger, feeling bored and desperate to go home. In later hospital stays, in a similarly post-operative state, but sometimes worse – unable to eat and subject to the unsatisfying gunk from the feeding tube, with that still-hungry feeling in the stomach, and knowing that Mum and Dad, Louis and Despina were all popping out for breakfast, lunch, afternoon tea, dinner – George would watch food programmes on TV. He would study the recipes of the grand chefs, the would-be grand chefs, the rank amateurs – all of them – intently, throughout the day. He was preparing himself for the joys of eating, the anticipation of a good meal, making his choice, savouring the flavours, discovering new recipes to try and, most importantly, just keeping in touch with a part of his identity – the love of food. He was still George; he was just George trapped in a bed. Unable to carry out the usual physical activities of being George, he would carry them out in his head, imagining, planning and above all, surviving. And this was what he was doing now.

At the end of two weeks he posted on Facebook "is finaly out of hospital. (early as usual) :D" – demonstrating, as he so often would, his pride at recovering quickly.

Mr Hyde had declared himself to be satisfied with the patient's progress and George was allowed home. The blood vessels joined to the muscle flap were pumping healthily, the wounds were healing and he was eating – albeit with fewer teeth than before – drinking and walking. He was walking with crutches, but on occasions he moved so fast that it was hard to keep up with him. In the next couple of weeks he began to bounce back to his old self, so happy that the tumour had been removed at last. Mum and Dad nearly had kittens when he played football with his cousins in his grandparents' little garden; they were terrified he would fall and do damage to his now fragile hip. But George brushed their fears aside, determined to forge his way ahead to recovery and get his life back.

However, a Facebook post a couple of weeks later records – "has fuckd his hip up a bit tryin to play footie. Not a good idea considerin its only been 3 weeks since he had a major operation on it :L"

He had plans. He planned to leave his old school once his GCSEs were completed and move on to a mixed sixth form in a girls' school, which he assumed would prove interesting for his social life. It would be a new life, with cancer left far behind him. He was full of life, of hope, of energy and enthusiasm.

---o---

At the end of two long weeks, the results of the pathology came through and they were called to an appointment with Mr Hyde at St George's. Dad, Mum and George made the tedious journey by car, one weekday morning in the rush hour. Dad was unbearably tense and extra impatient with the traffic, shouting unmentionables at irritating motorists, huffing and puffing at red traffic lights that held them up, sitting hunched and stiff in the driver's seat like a tightly wound spring. George was playing it cool as usual and Mum was trying to be supportive all round and keep Dad as calm as possible.

When they arrived, they parked in the hospital car park and made their way to the crowded maxillofacial clinic where they sat amongst the rows of patients waiting to be seen. Mum tried to read her book, George listened to his music, Dad sat fidgeting. When they were finally shown into Mr Hyde's room, nearly the whole surgical team was there, standing around the room at a respectful distance from the consultant and his patient. This was standard procedure; they were on hand if required, but otherwise it was 'speak when you are spoken to'.

Mr Hyde shook hands with George, Mum and Dad and pulled up his swivel chair close to the patient. He examined George's jaw briefly and asked how he had been. Then he came straight to the point; he was so sorry, but the histology showed that they had been unable to get a clear margin around the resected tumour. On one side, there was still evidence of live tumour cells in the margins of the resection. This suggested there might be some tumour cells left in George's jaw.

Dad collapsed in his chair with an "oh no!" the tears welling fast in his eyes. Mum gripped his arm fiercely, staring hard at his face to jolt him out of it, afraid of the effect it would have on George to see his father demonstrating such despair. He pulled himself together. George took it in slowly, turning it over in his mind with little show of emotion and then enquired what else could be done. Mr Hyde advised radiotherapy to mop up any tumour cells that might remain, although radiotherapy could cause some problems with the new bone. However, they should certainly see the radiotherapists and he definitely recommended they take this option because the consequences of not doing so could be worse than the threat to the bone. George dreaded radiotherapy; he knew it could cause new cancers in the future, especially given his gene disorder, his LFS. He knew that it might have caused the cancer he had now – correction; the cancer he still had now. There was to be no Facebook post on this day.

They left the room in a daze and wandered through the depressing corridors of the hospital until they came to a large area with a coffee bar set in the wall. There were seats around the outside of the space and a few tables and chairs in the middle. They stopped to buy a cup of tea, not because they especially wanted one, but simply to get their bearings. It was fairly crowded and they sat on the chairs against one of the walls, facing towards the individuals, couples and groups seated at the tables. George began to cry; he was frightened. They sat there, the three of them, with the world turned upside down again, their grief laid bare and plain for all to see, struggling to gain some equilibrium. Mum and Dad assured George they were not at the end of the road; there were plenty of options that Dad had researched. He would not be forced to have radiotherapy if he really didn't want it, but they should see the consultant radiotherapist and then make an informed decision. The fight was by no means over. Remember when he was three and there was still evidence of cancer cells in the margin and nothing came of it? It wasn't certain that any remaining cells would grow this time either. But they would gather all the information and then make a decision as to how to go forward. They would stay on the path facing the right way. The three of them gradually pulled themselves together, dried their tears, sipped their tea and left to find the car. They drove home, preparing to break the news to the rest of the family. George sat in the back with his headphones on, listening to his music. Mum and Dad were quiet in the front. Dad carried a dead weight in his heart. Somehow they had to go on.

For The Love of George

8. All Messed Up

George was growing into a young man. He was now nearly sixteen and as tall as his dad, although still very thin, especially since the rounds of chemotherapy. He had broad shoulders, long arms, somewhat thin wrists, but big hands with long, slim fingers. His legs were hairy and he had the shadow of a moustache on his upper lip and wispy 'bum-fluff' on his 'Desperate Dan' style chin. He had passed through the awkward stage, when parts of a boy's body seem to grow out of proportion to other parts and dress sense seems to be an alien concept. Now he was interested in clothes that fit his style. He dressed simply, in a fairly understated way, either in jogging bottoms and tee shirt or designer shirt and jeans, and he was building up a large selection of footwear that would eventually include Converse, Timberland boots and various types of pumps. He was fond of bling too, although he wasn't really a Chav. He would always select either a simple bracelet for his wrist or a chain for his neck to accompany his outfit. His favourite item was his silver dog tags on a chain, bought for him by Yiayia and

Buppou and, once his left ear was pierced, his large, diamanté ear stud. He had also entered the phase of perfumes and body sprays. Lynx 'Africa' would fill the house from top to bottom, or sometimes one of his more expensive perfumes – Guess 'Man' or Ben Sherman.

George walked with the fashionable unhurried stroll that involved dropping one knee very slightly with each two steps forward. He focused on being cool and laid back and usually succeeded, taking most things in his stride, leaving the fussing and faffing to others. Despite this, he would occasionally have an outburst of anger or frustration, which he would take out on the wall with his fist, but this was usually teenage hormone related. Once however, he became extremely angry when Mum rather forcefully accused him of being lazy after a round of chemo, and he tipped the contents of his bed over, barricading the door at the same time. He stayed curled up behind the door on his mattress until Mum could get the door open enough to apologise, smooth things over and get him and his bed back into some sort of order.

He was still a hero to his younger cousins. Auntie Ann's third daughter, Zoe, who was three years younger than George, had always adored him. He remained the leader of the gang of younger kids, even though some of them were several years his junior. He was big cousin George – the oldest of all the grandsons – who was always 'on' for a game of football or hide-and-seek or taking Auntie Ann's dog for a walk. They all loved him. He got on well with his two older cousins as well – Auntie Ann's two oldest girls. Nikki was three years older than him and he looked up to her as her younger sister did to him. He was always interested in what she was doing, especially as she was really good at sports and for a while had been in the Air Cadets, spending her weekends at camp and flying, before she grew up and went off to university. As his illness progressed, he was often visited by her older sister, Penny, and appreciated her company and her concern for him. She would bring DVDs and they would sit in his room watching them together. Yes, with George, it was like bees round a honey pot. At times, poor Louis struggled to get a look in – but the older boy was also big brother George to Louis. And he was younger brother to Despina, growing closer to her as he grew up, the two of them becoming really good friends.

Now George had to refocus himself on his cancer as things were not going according to plan. The operation was supposed to have taken care of things, allowing him to get ready for starting at a new school – a new beginning. Instead, he had to consider having a treatment that he was absolutely opposed to – radiotherapy. He was only too aware it was a treatment that could mess up his jaw, make him ill again, could cause him to have to go through all this again. He was thinking there was no way. It was all messed up. He hadn't had a proper life at school for nearly a year now. What else then? His dad would find something; he had to. Meanwhile, despite his feelings, he had to attend an appointment to meet the radiotherapist.

His Facebook post read "Might be gettin

Radiotherapy :@ FUCK THAT!!"

---o---

It was one afternoon in May that George, Mum and Dad drove to the Marsden to keep the appointment with the radiotherapist, or rather one of his registrars – and they were less than impressed. At first, they found it difficult to extract any useful facts from her, but eventually, after much questioning, gleaned several disturbing pieces of information. Firstly, it seemed there was a 50 percent chance of George developing a new cancer if he opted for radiotherapy – due to his Li Fraumeni Syndrome. Secondly, there was a 25% chance of the new jaw crumbling. As if this wasn't bad enough, there was no guarantee that the treatment would be successful; the registrar was not prepared to put a figure on the chances of success. Of course, there would be some side effects too – severe mouth ulceration, loss of saliva and trouble swallowing. The following week, they saw the consultant radiotherapist and the picture painted was similar.

George's Facebook post that evening read "is trying to make the hardest decision of his life nd cud so easily sick out on someone right now! :@."

In the end, George was adamant; he was not going to risk his new jaw crumbling or another cancer developing; he was not going to have radiotherapy and neither did he warm to the clinicians, which didn't help. Mum and Dad, although worried about declining the offer of treatment, were horrified by the prospect of the fall-out from it. No one was actually sure there were live cells left beyond the margins or that they would survive and grow. Alison, their oncologist, suggested they wait and see. They were grateful for her support in making this decision. Perhaps they were playing out in their minds a similar scenario to that which had come to pass when George was small, when there had been live malignant cells in the margins of his tumour resection, but the tumour hadn't re-grown and he had recovered. Perhaps they were thinking there would be a similar outcome this time. Was it just wishful thinking? It was a terrible decision to have to make and Mum and Dad agonised over it for several days, despite George's unequivocal response. They were just not sure that he fully understood the implications of the tumour re-growing and they were too afraid to tell him that his chances of survival would be severely diminished. Finally, they decided to support George in declining radiotherapy.

---o---

There followed more bad news. It transpired that the sample of resected tumour sent to Great Ormond St was too small for the requirements of the vaccine trial. The pathologists from St George's had mistakenly sent a biopsy sample size, which was inadequate for creating a vaccine. It was too late to rectify this, as there was no more live tumour available – and it had to be live. This put an end to George's chance of signing up for the trial, should the tumour grow again. Mum and Dad were incredulous and furious. Someone, somewhere had messed up – someone who didn't know that a child's life was at stake, or just didn't think. It wasn't clear at which point communication had broken down, but it was over now; the chance of joining the trial was ended and there was nothing that could be done. Dad sent some emails, expressing their concern that this should not happen to other patients in future, then they left it behind, moved on.

They asked their oncologist about other possible treatments, other trials that would be open to George. They knew these would not be standard treatments, and that they were into the area of the experimental, where cancer patients begin to look when all standard treatments have failed them, but Mum and Dad were convinced there were still options out there. Dad had kept up his research and he received relevant research papers on new trials and treatments every day.

Oh, the abundance of medical research! What terror it can instil in the layperson! And what hope it can also bring. There is research into this substance, research into that substance – research carried out in test tubes, in petri dishes, in mice, in rats and eventually various stages of clinical trials involving humans. Sometimes the results hit the headlines, "New cure for cancer! Blah, blah, blah..."

The press is often premature and misleading in its pronouncements. Mostly it transpires that whatever substance killed the tumours in the test tubes didn't go on to work in small mammals. Or if it worked in mammals, it didn't show much response in humans. And usually it took years to get to this point.

Mum and Dad knew that many things would

destroy a tumour in a test tube environment, outside the complexity of the body. Some treatments worked in small mammals too. And these were necessary steps, before attempting to administer potentially harmful substances to human beings. Even clinical trials in humans had to be done in stages, to ensure that doses were set at levels that would not cause great harm, whilst still proving effective. But proclamations made in the press were often in relation to the test tube stage, only very tiny steps on the way to looking for cures that might fizzle out into nothing. Mum and Dad knew that the media were irresponsible in their reporting of cancer research.

Dad's reading had taught them much about the sophistication of tumour cells – that a tumour is a complex system, an example of evolution in action; it survives by adapting. In the human body it creates great spaghetti junctions of blood vessels to support its survival; it can cannibalise surrounding healthy cells, set the host's immune system against normal cells, turn almost every harmful substance to its own advantage and eventually starve the host in its greed for sustenance – an evil, vicious, relentless, fighting force for survival. And so often it wins. It sends out its army of tiny cells to take up residence at other sites in the body; some scientists say it keeps them under strict control until it requires them to grow, which is likely to be when the main site is under attack or is resected. Then these metastases take over in the bid for survival of the cancer. As these new tumours grow larger, the patient becomes emaciated, organs are invaded and fail, the brain is infiltrated and ceases to function properly. And eventually, there is death to the patient.

Fortunately researchers all over the world are looking at different ways to tackle cancer, attempting to move on from the brutal treatments that kill healthy cells as well as cancer cells – the treatments that poison, burn or mutilate the patient's body. And yet, after over a hundred years of concerted effort in medical research there is still no guaranteed cure for this terrible disease, even with the most barbaric of treatments.

We all have potential cancers inside us: we have cells that mutate, but they are programmed to self-destruct, or our immune systems deal with them. Sometimes, however, they stay in our bodies for years, waiting for a chance to develop a blood supply and grow. Maybe healthy lifestyles help to avert a catastrophe, by keeping the cells dormant or enabling them to be destroyed. Certainly much has been written about the anti-cancer properties of certain foods and not just by cranks, but by highly-knowledgeable scientists and doctors. Berries contain polyphenols, brassicas contain glucosinolates, garlic and onions have allicin and, like apples, contain quercetin and anti-oxidant vitamins. Green tea contains catechins. There is resveratrol in red wine and lycopene in tomatoes. Many of these substances are anti-inflammatory; all of them support a healthy immune system. Dark chocolate, oily fish, citrus fruits, turmeric are all listed as potentially anti-cancer. Regular exercise makes its own contribution. Practices such as meditation that tackle the mind-set – the stresses that are imposed on our bodies through our minds – may have the potential to help keep us cancer-free. But they are clearly not the whole story. Hereditary factors, genes, play a role. Harmful substances, constant inflammation in the body, trauma to certain areas, may also play a part. George was dealt a terrible hand when he was born with a mutated TP53 gene and his body was unable to mount the usual defences against the onset of cancer.

There are those who blame the individual for developing cancer. They ask, "Did he smoke?" or, "Did she live an unhealthy lifestyle?" It is not the way forward. There is no humanity in such an approach. To err is to be human.

There are researchers who are beginning to regard cancer as a chronic condition, with a focus on controlling rather than curing the disease. Some researchers are looking at how to deprive a tumour of its ideal environment – to stop the maintenance of a blood supply, to destroy the acidity that a tumour thrives in, to prevent it from using surrounding cells for its own ends. If a cancer can be kept small, without a chance to invade surrounding organs or to metastasise, then it is not life-threatening. Some researchers believe that administering a powerful dose of chemotherapy from the outset is a mistake; only the weaker cells are killed, while the stronger cells adapt, become resistant. At this point, there are only less effective, secondary waves of chemical therapies available to doctors, to treat a stronger tumour.

An alternative approach is to give low doses of chemotherapy on a more frequent, sometimes daily, basis. At low doses many conventional chemotherapy drugs act to interfere with the process of angiogenesis by which tumours recruit a blood supply to get at the nutrients needed to survive and grow. Often these low-dose chemotherapy drugs are combined with anti-inflammatory drugs, which also attack the support systems used by the tumour. The reasoning behind this approach is that this form of treatment is not highly toxic to the patient and does not depress the patient's immunity, while it also has the potential to keep a tumour under control by depriving the cells of the conditions they need to thrive. Only time will tell whether these metronomic therapies will become more mainstream and whether they will prove to be effective.

Meanwhile societies turn to screening, with the assurance that early detection means more chance of survival. It seems to make sense. But even this apparently useful approach is surrounded by controversy, particularly in relation to breast cancer. Whilst it is widely acknowledged that breast screening is beneficial for individuals suffering from cancer predisposition syndromes, there are an increasing number of researchers who regard screening as inappropriate for wider sections of the female population. They point out that, although some women benefit from early detection through screening, many more are unnecessarily treated for cancers that will not develop into life-threatening diseases during their lifetimes. As oncologists cannot tell which lumps will turn into life-threatening cancers and which will either disappear or fail to develop, it is obviously regarded as ethical to treat all lumps as though they were dangerous – with mastectomy, radiotherapy and chemotherapy – resulting in considerable trauma to those women.

For the lay individual looking for a cure, it is a minefield. In addition to the contradictory evidence in medical science, there are the cranks and charlatans – parasites who will charge the desperate cancer patient huge sums of money to provide a so-called cure that is less than worthless. Lifetime savings are spent, houses are re-mortgaged and still there is no cure forthcoming.

Dad waded through all this, trying to make sufficient sense of it to take decisions about what might help his son. He spent hours in a day reading, turning over in his mind, discussing with Mum, contacting doctors, researchers, professors, and emailing medical journal papers to their oncologist, before deciding whether to give George particular treatments. Not all of the medical research focused on potentially harmful substances. Many involved treatments that were already used for other conditions such as diabetes, worms, mouth ulceration. Often these were over-the-counter supplies, considered harmless enough that any adult could pick them up at a small cost. And yet these drugs were being seriously looked at by medical researchers as potential inhibitors of tumour growth. Dad came across a medical trial in India, looking at curcumin, an anti-inflammatory substance found in the spice turmeric, and he received advice on a suitable dose for George. He bought Omega 3 capsules that were being shown to be highly anti-inflammatory, potentially making conditions more difficult for tumour cells to thrive. He discovered that some people were treating cancer with low-carbohydrate diets and, although Mum and Dad never subjected George to a strict ketogenic diet, as it was called, they did try and adopt a fairly low-carb diet on a day-to-day basis. This involved substituting cauliflower or swede mash for potatoes, parsnip chips for potato chips, using a sweetener derived from the plant stevia to sweeten desserts and increasing their protein, fat and vegetable intake. There were many more substances that Dad invested in for George over the months and the cupboard under the stairs in the family home was full to bursting with pots and boxes of capsules, tablets, powders, all jumbled up in various bigger boxes and bags. Dad even invested in a capsule maker, so that he could make his own capsules.

One day, when Dad and George were away in hospital and Louis was at school, Mum decided to clear out the cupboard and repack everything with an inventory for each box. In that way they could find what they needed much more easily. She had pulled everything out into the hallway, not only the various bags, boxes, pots, bottles of supplies they had purchased, but also bandages, dressings, anti-sickness pills etc given to them by the hospital. Every inch of the floor was covered, from the foot of the stairs to the kitchen door.

There was a ring on the doorbell. Mum froze in horror, then went to the door and opened it tentatively – just a few inches – and came face to face with a man wishing to read the gas meter. The gas meter was in the cupboard under the stairs.

Mum was embarrassed. "Can you come back

later? It's not convenient at the moment."

Apparently not; the man was insistent it must be done then and there. There was nothing for it; Mum asked him to wait a moment. She pushed the front door to, quickly gathered up as many boxes etc as she could and shoved them into the sitting room. Then she let him in. He stepped carefully over the many remaining boxes and stooped down to read the meter in the cupboard. On his way out he looked at Mum quizzically, but she avoided his gaze, said a quick thank-you and shut the front door. Then she burst into a fit of giggles. Later, Louis laughed too, at the thought of Mum looking like the biggest hypochondriac in town.

And so Mum and Dad continued to search for cures for George. In the meantime, George was on study leave from school – not that he'd been able to be at school much since the operation, and even study leave was interspersed with hospital appointments. Their oncologist referred them to the leading clinician and researcher in osteosarcoma in the UK, to see if he had anything to offer in the way of trials that George might be eligible to join. Oncologists often seemed to defer to this learned man on the subject, but for George, nothing was forthcoming. He was not easy to talk to either, and seemed arrogant to Mum, Dad and George.

During this time George revised for his GCSEs as best he could, given how tired he often felt. He needed the usual push from Mum and Dad, but he was probably not especially unusual as a teenage boy in this respect. He attended appointments for scans, the results of which showed no change, his Hickman line was removed as there was no further chemotherapy planned and he attended appointments with Alison at the Marsden and with Mr Hyde at St George's. Life went on, while they all waited and watched. He had effectively left school now, apart from the impending exams and his Facebook page recorded his goodbyes:

"Southborough '04 – '09, the 5 most jokes years of my life xD Good luck to all u Southborough legends!"

And at the end of May he announced: "is alowd to play footy now, Woooo!!"

Meanwhile, he had been nagging Dad silly about finding him a dog.

9. It's a Dog's Life

George had wanted a Staffordshire terrier, like Auntie Ann's dog, Lola. Mum and Dad however, weren't too fond of the idea; they thought it was ugly and badly behaved.

"Well, it's true," thought Louis (who was perhaps influenced by his fear of dogs). Lola jumped all over the furniture and didn't do as she was told.

But George loved the dog. And of course to a teenage boy Staffs were cool. Unfortunately, Mum and Dad were not to be moved; Staffs were out. A medium-sized dog was ok – not huge, mind – and thank goodness nobody wanted a yappy little dog. At least there was some agreement there.

As a kid, Mum had had a Border Collie cross and so she suggested a Border. Everyone liked the idea – sort of. But George wasn't sure and he continued to look at other breeds on the Internet. One moment he was keen on a chocolate Labrador, but then he thought about a black Labrador instead. Next, he saw a Canaan on the web, which looked like a cross between a Border and a Husky, with short hair. They all thought it was lovely, but Canaans came from Israel and the parents weren't sure about getting a dog that came from a hot country. And so the hunt for the right dog continued and no one was certain what they would actually end up with.

One day, when Yiayia and Buppou came over, the family played a trick on Yiayia, telling her that George had chosen his dog and had a picture of it on his computer. She was very excited for him, even though she couldn't really stand dogs. She thought they were dirty – well so they are! Later, when they had acquired their dog, and the boys stayed at her house with it, she would make them wash their hands every time they touched it. George loved to wind her up by kissing the dog in front of her.

Buppou, on the other hand, didn't mind dogs. He told a good story about Yiayia and a dog. One day, when they lived in Brixton and the eldest of Dad's three sisters was still a teenager and living at home, they were going out. Buppou had gone on ahead to unlock the car, when suddenly he heard lots of screaming and Yiayia and her daughter came running round the corner chased by a little dog. They were terrified. The funny point about this story that amused the boys greatly was that each time Buppou told it, the dog got smaller. And every time he told it Yiayia would make the dog bigger. If Yiayia said the dog was up to her waist and barking fiercely, Buppou said it was only knee-high and yapping like a little terrier! The truth probably lay somewhere in between, but the boys loved to hear them argue about it. The bigger Yiayia made the dog, the smaller Buppou said it was. In the end, it seemed the dog would end up being bigger than a person or smaller than a mouse. Given his fear of dogs, the latter sounded good to Louis. Meanwhile he and George would play a joke of their own.

George had found a photo on the Internet, of a huge, gnarled, slavering and fierce-looking dog and he proudly showed it off to their grandmother. Mum, Dad and the boys could hardly contain themselves when they saw her face, as she tried to act pleased for George.

"It's a bit big agabimou," she said, using her usual Greek term of endearment.

At this point they all rolled around laughing. Yiayia took the joke well and was much more impressed when she saw the photo of the real dog.

The actual dog chosen? Well, Mum and Dad had won out with the Border Collie. Dad had been in touch with a rescue centre in Ascot, asking for a dog of around a year old, as he had been advised this would be easier to handle than a Border puppy. George had then begun to nag him constantly, until finally, during GCSE study leave, they learnt that the centre had a one-year-old male, which had been picked up in Wales. It was friendly, well-behaved, considered calm for a Border and appeared to have been neutered.

George posted on Facebook, "is goin to see the dog he mite be gettin, on Saturday."

In the meantime, his younger brother was struggling with his fear. Louis had agreed to getting a dog for George's sake, but the reality of knowing there was now a specific animal waiting for them sent cold shivers down his back. Agreeing to something in theory was not the same as dealing with it in reality. And now the day had arrived when they were going to meet the dog that might soon be theirs. He breathed a sigh of relief, however, when Mum and Dad said they wouldn't be bringing the creature back with them that day, as George still needed to get his last GCSE exam out of the way. Only after that would they fetch the pooch – if it was the right dog.

And so it was that one Saturday afternoon in June they set off in the Zafira to drive to Ascot to meet the dog. George appeared as cool as ever, although in reality he was only just suppressing his excitement. He had been waiting for this day for months. The thought of his own 'best friend' had kept him going through the bad times and he couldn't wait to take his dog to the park and show him off to his mates. When they reached the centre, they pulled into a long drive and came to a standstill by a small shelter of some kind. George got out with Mum and Dad and pressed a bell to make contact with the staff inside the main building, while Louis sat in the back of the car and tried to calm himself. A few minutes later a woman came walking out of the gate with a black and white Border on a lead. The dog was quite a picture: it had a beautiful shiny, black and white coat that had obviously been bathed and thoroughly brushed, a handsome black face with a flash of white down the middle and velvety ears that pricked up immediately it spied its potential new owners. It was quite tall for a Border and it began jumping about excitedly.

"Christ, it's a bit lively!" said Louis, peering through a small gap at the top of the car window.

The poor younger boy was overwhelmed with fear and he felt tears welling up. All he could think then was how the hell was he going to do this? Did they actually know how hard it was for him?

George, Mum and Dad however, were beaming. Dad went rushing towards it the moment he set eyes on it.

"Oh what a lovely dog!"

Louis was not impressed.

Was this his dad? Who preferred animals on a plate with two veg? Dad, who sent his kids out into the garden to throw buckets of cold water over any cat that dared cross the threshold? Who even told the boys to kick cats? And here he was – gushing like a girl. Well, you never really knew a person... Later on his dad would deny this initial reaction, but Mum would continue to tease him about it for years.

George was a natural with the dog; he moved towards it with a broad smile of utter happiness on his face, stroked its head and spoke to it gently, taking the lead from the member of staff, to go for a little walk round the grounds. When his older brother returned, Louis managed to emerge from the car and, taking special care to keep a good distance, took a photo of the animal sitting upright and happy, leaning against George's legs. The photo, later posted on Facebook, showed George, looking every bit the new owner, proud and smiling in his jeans and hoodie, his mop of coarse, curly hair that had grown again since the chemo blowing wildly in the wind.

The relief came over Louis in a huge wave when they finally set off again in the car to go home, but the deal was done. They were to return the following week to pick up the Border Collie. So, it was final. Louis was aware that all eyes were on him. Was he going to chicken out? No bloody way, not after all this. Somehow he would do it.

"It was just the shock," he told them. "I'll be alright next time."

The only problem was the staff at the centre had named the dog Zhivago.

"What a stupid name for a dog!" sneered George, and they all agreed on that.

"Can you imagine calling him in the park? Zhivago! Here boy!" laughed Dad.

Fortunately it was only a temporary name and consequently, on the journey home they all set about finding an alternative. There were several ridiculous suggestions, from Fido to Finkelstein, but George had just the right name up his sleeve. "Flash," he said, with that quiet George kind of confidence; and the name stuck. He had chosen the name because of the flash of white down the dog's face.

The following Saturday they picked up Flash.

George posted on Facebook, "has his new dog sittin right next to him (smiley face)"

They brought Flash home in the back of the car. Louis was jumpy because the dog was constantly moving around behind him, but George turned round and gently but firmly encouraged the nervous and excited creature to keep his distance from the younger boy.

At the house Flash was shown into the garden, where he commenced to nose around excitedly. Then he tried to poo on the flowerbeds and Mum began enthusiastically directing him towards a patch of ground covered in ivy, behind the trampoline. The dog was confused – not surprisingly. Over the next few weeks he became even more confused about where to poo, when Mum and Dad realised that they didn't really want any part of their back garden turned into a dog toilet. George couldn't see what all the fuss was about and thought they should just leave him to go where he wanted, as long as it was outside – not that George was first in line to pick up the neat pile of steaming turds in the little black plastic poo bags. Somehow he managed to just not be around for that one. Finally, Flash was directed to 'do his business' at the side of the house, in the driveway in front of the garage. Here it was easy to clean up and the area could be hosed down regularly.

Over the weeks that followed, Mum constructed ridiculous barriers to attempt to prevent Flash from getting into the back garden when the back door – located near the back corner of the house past the back gate – was open, or to stop him from running out into the road at the front of the house where there was no gate at all. Her attempts were pretty ineffective and in the end, when the grass at the back was covered in bare patches from the salty dog pee, Mum brought in a carpenter to construct a small, picket-style gate beyond the back door, at the rear corner of the house. This meant that Flash couldn't get into the back garden unless he was 'invited'. A double gate was also positioned at the front edge of the house, so that he was contained effectively at the side of the house. Here he could pee and poo to his heart's content and also play football with the boys – after the poo had been picked up that is. Fortunately, as time passed and he grew up, he stopped doing anything toilet related at home and saved it for his walks. Mum was impressed with his bladder's ability to hold its water for a good ten hours. She wished the other males were as efficient when the family was on long car journeys.

The day after collecting the dog, George posted on Facebook:

"Flash is the most bangin dog ever (smiley face)"

Despite this enthusiastic beginning, all did not go well in the weeks that followed. Facebook records George being woken up at 5 a.m. by the dog, also of getting soaked giving him a bath and, whilst he may not have expressed much irritation to his friends, he was becoming somewhat downhearted about progress in training his dog. There were also the first tiresome weeks of cleaning up wee and poo in the house, trying to stop Flash from chewing the furniture and attempting to get him to obey basic commands. It was hard work. George was disappointed, feeling that Flash was a slow learner. Mum and Dad knew it took time and patience to train a dog and that the dog was clearly very intelligent, but even they felt weighed down with the effort. None of them suspected that Flash was actually much younger than they had been told. One family dinnertime Louis became very upset when Dad suggested that maybe it would be better to return Flash to the rescue centre, before he became too attached to them. George was tending to agree. Mum wasn't too keen, given that Flash had been abandoned once already in his life; it just didn't seem fair. But Louis was furious and upset. After all he'd been through to come to terms with getting a dog he couldn't believe they would actually consider sending it back. He made his feelings felt.

"No way!"

Get a dog for George's sake, go through all of that trauma and have to adjust to living with a big, hairy, excitable creature with a potentially lethal set of gnashers! You must be bloody joking! The dog was staying.

In the end Flash stayed by default, as they kept putting off the decision and it was eventually too late to do anything about it. Then the family learnt from the vet that their protégé was younger than they had been told and this helped to get things in perspective.

George posted his reaction on Facebook, "'s dog is only 6-8 months old and hasnt been neutered according to the vet, which means the rescue place we got him from are complete fails cos they said he was one year old and was neutered. They deserve a clap."

Thankfully, Flash settled down and George realised it took time to train a dog. He was actually a very smart dog and would learn many commands as time passed. George loved to play fetch with him, and Louis was the first to teach him to jump on to the trampoline. Flash soon became a part of the family and seemed very happy with the new home he had found.

There was, however, one problem that gave increasing cause for concern: Flash needed a good deal of exercise. As Dad took the car to work and they lived a fair distance from anywhere the animal could run free, finding time to fit in walks created something of a strain. And although George wasn't quite as keen on walking his dog as he had imagined he would be, he also needed to be careful how much strain he put on his hip. As the weeks passed and he became less mobile and hospital appointments made new demands on their time and energy, they were forced to employ a dog walker to take on some of the walks.

Georgina was an energetic blond woman of the same age as Dad. She loved dogs, had been walking them for years and helped the family to handle Flash. Although she rewarded him with a large bonio biscuit every day, any bad behaviour would result in firm treatment and on-lead walks. He loved her to bits. In the morning, five minutes before she arrived, he would be sitting bolt upright by the front door, tail wagging.

During this time, Louis actually came to feel Flash was the best pooch around and definitely deserving of his name. He was smart, fast, cute – what more could you want? He learnt some good commands too – 'sit', 'paw', 'round', 'down', 'run', 'touch' and others. He came back when his name was called or when he was whistled. His favourite game was 'fetch the stick'. He would play for hours on walks and find tennis balls all the time, sniffing them out in even the deepest undergrowth. As time went by, even Despina grew to really love Flash.

In the beginning, Flash loved George; after all, he was George's dog. George loved to cuddle and stroke him and to secretly feed him scraps under the dinner table when he thought Mum wasn't looking. In that way, he made sure his dog always sat next to him at the table. It made Louis mad that when George saw him stroking Flash or playing with him he would call the dog away and Flash would just go. It was another one of those ways that George asserted his big brother status over Louis. And it infuriated the younger boy. Even Mum found herself rising to the bait and competing with George for Flash's attention.

And so Flash settled into family life. He became the family dog, as much as George's, and over time he became a good guard dog, making Mum and Louis feel secure and looked after when Dad and George were away in hospital. He was an early warning system for any invasion of the territory by humans, foxes, squirrels, pigeons and even frogs. He also had constant arguments with an annoying local dog, who was always barking. Mum thought maybe the other dog was just alerting Flash to the presence of foxes in the area, but Dad was convinced it was a case of establishing who had the larger testicles – even after Flash's had been removed.

The year progressed: George finished exams and school for the summer; dog walks took place on lazy sunny days. George's Hickman line had been removed and he turned sixteen.

On Facebook he reflected, "will have had: 3 different types of cancer, 17 operations, 13 scars, 22 different vitamins, 7 chemotherapy drugs, 3 very powerful anti sickness drugs, 2 very powerful pain killers and one pretty fucked up genetic disorder by the time he is 16/17."

Around this time, Despina graduated from her PGCE course. Proud of her achievement during such a difficult time, she invited Dad and George to attend her graduation ceremony and share the occasion with her. One sunny afternoon in July, the three of them set off in the Zafira to drive down to Guildford Cathedral for the ceremony. There was an optimistic feeling in the air and, during the journey, Despina made a point of talking to George about student life, about moving away from home and becoming independent.

They all wondered what George would do once he had completed his A levels. As they chatted, they made a definite effort to focus on the positive, to try not to think about the horrible things that might still lie ahead for him. He said he had liked Surrey University when Despina had taken him there, and he liked the idea that his dad had a connection with the place (he had studied for his PhD there and he worked nearby). The only problem was he wasn't exactly sure what he wanted to do, except he was quite keen on studying something in computer graphics or robotics, although they weren't subjects on offer at Surrey. It was a good conversation, thinking about the future in a positive way, given all that

George had been through since the disease had been diagnosed.

After the ceremony, they had photos taken outside the cathedral. One photo, of a smiling and proud father with his two children in the sunshine, showed a relaxed-looking George, his arm draped affectionately over his sister's shoulder, a picture of health aside from the swelling on one side of his face. It was a picture that expressed hope somehow – for a better future, a happier life ahead. Yes, university was definitely something George wanted to experience, and he'd been saving money for it for some time. All it needed now was some hard work to get A levels and for his cancer to disappear once and for all.

The hope for a new, good life continued: George and Louis went for a dog walk early one Saturday morning. Although it was August and holidays were beckoning, the air was still a little crisp, despite the English summer sun poking through. As they strolled along in the park together, with Flash fetching the sticks they were throwing for him, they discussed the future. They talked about how, once the cancer had been dealt with, George would go off to university and then he'd get a job and have his own flat and car. He would drive home and pick up Louis, who would be a teenager by then and at a new school studying for his own future. George would take Louis to stay in his flat and they would have a good time, away from home, doing their own thing. They chatted in this way, brother-to-brother, with George outlining the future that he so hoped would come to pass.

---o---

The reality was that George was no longer receiving any treatment. To this end, Dad had been in touch with a consultant at University College Hospital (UCH) in London, who treated cancer patients with something called photodynamic therapy (PDT). In fact, he was a pioneer of this therapy in the UK. They asked Alison to refer George to him, which she did, the aim being to find out if this treatment would be an option for George, in the event that the tumour on his jaw was to grow again.

The procedure involved injecting a light-sensitive drug, called a photosensitiser, into a patient and then waiting for the drug to accumulate in the tumour cells (normal cells wouldn't take up the drug to the same extent). Once the drug had been absorbed by the tumour, light from a laser or LED would be applied to the cells through a surgical procedure. The photosensitive drug would react to the light and in the process kill the tumour cells. In this way PDT could be used to destroy solid tumours directly. After treatment, the patient would be light-sensitive and need to stay out of sunlight or strong artificial light for a couple of weeks, in order to avoid burns. The doctor concerned, who was a specialist in head and neck surgery, had had some success with this treatment and George, Dad and Mum felt it was well worth investigating.

Therefore they made the journey to busy Tottenham Court Rd in central London one weekday afternoon in August 2009 to keep an appointment with the consultant. The appointment was to be held in an old annexe located in a side street, the main hospital building being a huge modern, glass structure on the corner of Euston Road. They climbed the narrow flights of stairs in the old building – as Mum didn't like small lifts – and took a seat in a cramped, busy, packed waiting-area. It seemed that appointments were running an hour or so late. Whilst this wasn't unusual, neither was it welcome news. Consequently, they were pleasantly surprised when, after only ten or fifteen minutes, the consultant came out, introduced himself and asked them to follow him to his consulting room.

The consultant was a very personable man, who spoke directly to George, who immediately warmed to him, as did Mum and Dad. He asked how George was doing and how he was feeling about taking up new treatment offers. Then, after explaining the PDT procedure he confirmed that he could certainly operate on George, should the tumour return. They left feeling encouraged by the knowledge that the treatment was a viable option and that they could book appointments directly in future.

In the meantime, Alison had offered George an experimental immunotherapy treatment called interferon. Although this would require him to inject himself each day for a period of eighteen months, he was reassured by the knowledge that the small needle would only pierce the body subcutaneously. The treatment would probably cause some flu-like symptoms in the first couple of weeks, but this would wear off. They all felt it was worth a try. At least now they could start their summer holidays in the knowledge that something was being done.

The day after the appointment at UCH, Mum and Dad were speeding down the M20, on their way to Normandy for their second holiday alone – a week in a cottage in the French countryside. George and Louis had been dropped off at Yiayia and Buppou's and were heading off to Center Parcs with their grandparents, plus Despina, aunts, Uncle David and cousins. George and Louis were very excited. Mum and Dad were excited too because they were going to have a quiet week to themselves to relax and recharge their batteries, knowing that George would be well looked after by the family and that he would also be sensible about eating healthily. Of course, they would never stop him from being reckless at physical activities, especially when it came to bike riding…

At Center Parcs, the boys, Despina, the aunts, Uncle David and cousins took bikes to get around the site. Louis had finally mastered riding a bike, helped by Despina, after some years of wobbling around precariously in the saddle. George, though, was a 'pro', and had been a natural at it from a young age. At Centre Parcs, he sped wildly around the lanes and through the woods. He also took great delight in skidding to a halt in front of other cyclists, suddenly braking, swerving and turning abruptly into the path of whichever unsuspecting person was in the saddle of the bike next to him – usually Despina. She found this action infuriating and it was the source of much irritation between them. He, of course, carried on regardless and continued to throw himself with complete abandon into every activity. All in all everyone had a great time. Louis said he particularly enjoyed the crazy roller skating disco and sitting up late in the log cabin occupied by his aunts and cousins, before returning with Despina and George, to sleep next door in the cabin they shared with Yiayia and Buppou. It seemed that it was good times once again.

Mum and Dad spent a week lazing about and reading in their cottage in Normandy, as well as going for pleasant walks and strolls around the country lanes. They picked blackberries and plums, which Mum made into endless jars of jam to take home. And they consumed plenty of wine and good food while sitting outside, chatting and gazing at the view over the rolling countryside; there were still good things in life. If only George could be cured, then life would be almost perfect.

For The Love of George

10. Endeavour and Achievement: In the Face of Adversity

The family returned from their holidays refreshed and relaxed, but two weeks later the tension was mounting once more. George was due to have his second MRI scan since his operation, and they were understandably nervous about the outcome. On Friday 21st August 2009 Dad and George drove to the Marsden for the scan, but they were not expecting to get the results for a few days.

When they set off in the morning, Mum and Louis stayed at home to prepare for the annual week away in Southwold. The four of them would be leaving the next day and there was still plenty of packing to complete. By lunchtime, however, bed linen, towels, supplies of food – human and dog – were all in bags and boxes by the front door, and clothes had been sorted into neat piles ready to pack.

"Order from chaos," proclaimed Mum.

"Can we stop now?" said Louis.

At the Marsden, George had his MRI scan and then waited for his appointment with Alison in her Friday clinic. In the children's unit, where the day clinics were held, Alison's clinic seemed to be running even later than usual. Finally, George was the last patient waiting, sitting with Dad on the chairs outside Alison's room. Dad could see that there was a lot of activity. Doctors were coming in and out, Alison was on the phone and there was something in the air that told Dad bad news was on the way. The longer they waited the more convinced he became that there was something wrong. George, who was his usual cool self, playing on his PSP, told his frantic father to calm down.

Meanwhile, at home after lunch, Mum and Louis set off with Flash for Home Park, an extensive stretch of walled-in, deer-inhabited land that runs along the north side of the River Thames at Kingston, all the way to Hampton Court Palace. Although they were concerned about George, they knew they wouldn't get the results of the scan that day, and so they set off with a view to enjoying the walk. It was a warm, breezy day, with typical fluffy white clouds punctuating a blue sky and they picked up ice creams along the way, from the little café by the river. It was a half-hour walk to get to the park – along the river into Kingston on their side, and then over the bridge to where the park started on the other side. Since the creation of Charter Quay in Kingston, with its many restaurants and bars, the river was permanently busy during the summer months. The ice creams were compensation for struggling through the crowds, with Flash desperate to get off the lead and run free.

In Home Park they released the dog from his leash and watched him bound away. They stopped to allow him to swim in one of the large ponds, throwing sticks out on to the water for him to fetch. Mum and Louis loved to watch the muscles of his shoulders rise and fall, as he forged his way through the water. After that he had a good half-hour run in the long grass and by the time they left the park he was panting loudly. They were just crossing back over busy Kingston Bridge when Mum's mobile rang: it was Dad. She struggled to hear him over the traffic noise, but she could tell he was in a terrible state.

Once they were over the bridge and Mum could hear better, the picture emerged more clearly. George and Dad had finally been seen by Alison and one of her registrars. She had informed them that the MRI had already been reported and had confirmed Dad's fears that there was bad news; there was recurrent disease in the jaw. There was no doubt about it, as it had already grown to around two centimetres. It was clear the interferon wasn't working, and therefore she was planning to terminate the treatment. George had wanted to know what would happen next. What other treatment would he be offered? Alison had assured him there were still options to explore and an appointment at UCH should be made, with a view to going ahead with PDT. They should also see Mr Hyde again, to explore the possibility of another operation. Dad had found it hard to cope without Mum there. He hadn't expected to receive bad news on the same day as the scan. He had just not been prepared for it. He was trying to remain upbeat about the alternatives still open to George, but on the phone to Mum he was distraught. Mum's heart sank; she hadn't been expecting this news either. Dad said they were leaving the hospital immediately; Mum told Louis and they rushed home to be there when Dad and George arrived.

At home, Mum and Dad discussed the situation. It wasn't just the news that the tumour had returned that had devastated Dad. It was the fact that it was already two centimetres across. This was a considerable amount to have grown in the nine weeks since the last CT scan and it implied that the tumour was vigorous and fast growing. The next step was to find out if the cancer had metastasised as well. Accordingly, a bone-scan and CT scans of the pelvis and chest were planned for the following week. They could still go to Southwold, but it would mean returning after only a few days.

Mum and Dad were worried about Alison's decision to take George off the interferon. He had only started the treatment three-and-a-half weeks previously. What if it was actually slowing the growth of the tumour? How could they be sure that growth wouldn't accelerate if the treatment stopped? Alison, however, was convinced from her experience that it would have prevented re-growth if it had been working – or at the very least the tumour wouldn't have grown back so fast. The treatment would be terminated and George would be referred to Mr Hyde for a discussion about further surgery. George posted on Facebook:

"was just informed that there is another tumour growing inside him. Woo-FUCKING-hoo!!!"

Meanwhile, they had a few days away to recover from the news and think things through.

The next morning they set off for Southwold, but their brief stay was clouded by the knowledge of the recurrence. George was quieter than usual and Dad was clearly worried. Despite this, on Tuesday evening before they were due to return home, the four of them sat down to a meal together in 'The Crown', an old hotel and pub that served superb food in an informal setting. It was an expensive treat and they enjoyed the meal, especially George, who gained enormous pleasure from the perfectly-prepared rare duck breast. Then, the next day, with heavy hearts, they journeyed back to Kingston to face the implications of a new stage in George's disease.

On Thursday, Dad drove George to his old school to pick up his GCSE results. Amazingly, he had managed to achieve an A grade in Science, a subject he had studied almost solely in hospital. He had also gained some B's and C's, which considering the huge disruption to his schooling, was a job well done and Dad was very proud of him. They set off for the girls' school a few miles away, where George was to enrol in the mixed sixth form.

George's world was once again collapsing in on him. He had planned for a new start, a new set of friends, a branching out into a new social situation, cancer-free. His sister, when she was his age, had stayed at her old school to study for her A levels, but George wanted to be adventurous, to move on. Now it was all falling apart. He would start a new school and goodness only knows when he would be able to attend. Dad wondered what was going through his son's head. George was not one to voice his feelings very often, even when asked, which made it all the more affective when he did, but for now he was saying little. Determined as ever though, he signed up for his chosen subjects – Maths, Biology, Chemistry and Psychology. Then it was home for a quick lunch, before setting off with Mum, Dad and Louis, for an appointment with Mr Hyde.

---o---

At St George's, Mr Hyde welcomed them into his room, examined George, expressed his disappointment that they hadn't opted for radiotherapy, then quickly put that aside to focus on the current situation. He had studied the scans and concluded that it was feasible to operate once again. However, before doing so, he would require George to have another biopsy. This was necessary, he informed them, in order to confirm that it was tumour showing on the scan and not some other trauma to the area. Although the latter was unlikely, it was always possible. His intention, meanwhile, was to schedule the operation for Monday 14th September – just over two weeks away. As the family had private health insurance through Dad's work, he would also investigate the possibility of carrying out the surgery in St. Anthony's, a private hospital just half an hour's drive from the family home. Permission had been refused by the hospital the first time round, as George had been under sixteen, but now that George had passed his sixteenth birthday, Mr Hyde was hopeful permission would be forthcoming. There was some relief for George in this knowledge.

Over the next week George suffered with a stiff jaw and back pain. He was not in a good mood, as his Facebook post records:

"seriously feels like killing someone atm :@"

On Friday he attended an induction at his new school, after which he reported that he had met some young people he could imagine being friends with. Mum and Dad thought that was an encouraging start. His Facebook post was more enthusiastic:

"thinks Coombe tday was toooo sikk!!!"

Immediately after the school induction, they made their way over to St George's once again – this time for the biopsy. As expected, the histology confirmed the presence of tumour. Six days later, on Thursday 10th September, they attended another appointment with Mr Hyde, for a pre-operative assessment and a more detailed discussion of the procedure for the new operation.

This time, Mr Hyde proposed that bone be taken from George's fibula to create a new section of jaw. The required muscle would come from his upper back, as would the blood vessels that would be pulled round to connect to the muscle flap, once it was wrapped around the new jaw. There would be a whole new set of scars and more trauma to the facial nerves but, despite this, George was keen to proceed in the hope that all of the tumour would be removed this time, even though he would be going into hospital on the first day of actual school. They went home feeling a little more hopeful, if somewhat daunted by the thought of more surgery.

Somehow George dealt with all this. He was a

boy of few words, reserving his vocal interjections for well-timed wisecracks, or sharp little understatements that seemed to sum up a whole plethora of feelings and always hit the nail on the head. When not being examined by doctors or the subject of their diagnoses and prognoses, which would provoke single word answers from him, he could be found with his headphones on, listening to music – dubstep, techno, drum and bass – watching a DVD, playing a combat game on his Xbox or surfing the Internet. If he was worried he would not express it; he would brood until he could contain it no longer and then everything would come out in a few fraught sentences, perhaps even accompanied by tears.

And so it was that later that same evening George came down to the sitting room and complained about his knee; it was swollen and he said it felt stiff. He was worried and wanted to have it looked at. In typical George style, he had been brooding on it for a number of hours before deciding to tell Mum and Dad. Dad was worried. Mum suggested they went to the Marsden. It was four days before the scheduled operation.

The next day, Friday, Dad and George visited the Marsden, where George was examined and an MRI scan of the knee was taken. Once again, they waited at the hospital, this time knowing they would get the scan results; and once again the news was bad. The scan showed an abnormal mass that was interpreted as being tumour. The implications were enormous. The likelihood was that the disease was now metastatic, which created a whole new patient profile for George.

By Saturday the swelling had miraculously reduced, but the visit the day before had set in motion machinery that could not or would not be reversed. The operation, due to take place on Monday, was cancelled. It was considered inappropriate to operate on the primary tumour site if metastases had appeared, as there was no knowing how many times it might be necessary to operate to tackle sprouting tumours. Once a patient had metastases the whole prognosis changed, bringing with it a new set of ethical dilemmas. Metastatic osteosarcoma implied that the patient would almost certainly die from the disease, and it would be unethical to keep cutting a person who was not going to live. This wasn't actually spelled out in so many words, but it was the message implied. Fortunately, George didn't appear to have picked up on it. Or had he? Either way, there would be no operation. Mum regretted ever having suggested they go to the Marsden to have the knee checked out.

A week later and several scans and X-rays later, George was started on a new chemotherapy protocol, with a combination of the drugs gemcitabine and docetaxel, which were often used to treat breast cancer. The drugs caused tiredness and some tingling in his fingers, but were otherwise well-tolerated – at least at first. Hospital appointments still involved a lot of waiting around, as George noted on Facebook:

"cant believe how incompitent the hospital were today. My appointment was at 11 and I managed to get out at 4:30 lol"

George was also anticipating with some

trepidation, going back to school following chemo –
"wishing that people wont laugh or stare at me on
monday cos of the lack of hair lol"

And he was perhaps regretting just a little having
left his old school:

"just got back from taking his brother to the
southborough open evening, it kinda makes me wna go
back lol"

For Mum and Dad, the next move was to book an
appointment at University College Hospital with a view
to proceeding with PDT. This was done, the appointment
kept and the wait for a surgery date for PDT – on the jaw
initially – began. Mum and Dad were keen to move
things along fast, but it was not to be. The wheels of
hospital machinery seemed to turn so slowly at times, as
if there was no urgency at all. The jaw surgery had been
cancelled in a flash, but it was nearly two months later
that George was finally admitted to UCH for an injection
of photosensitive dye.

---o---

Dad and George made their way to UCH on the
train on Friday 6th November 2009. The plan was for
George to have the dye injected on Friday and stay in
hospital over the weekend, until the procedure was
carried out on Tuesday. Mum and Louis would visit over
the weekend. However, when Dad and George arrived
they were shown to a room on a children's ward, where
the nurses seemed unfamiliar with the whole process of
preparing for PDT. After the injection, George was
unnerved once again by the seeming incompetence of

some hospital nursing staff and he was adamant that he wanted to go home until the day of the procedure. Perhaps he wasn't confident that their knowledge was sufficient to protect him from acquiring burns from too high light levels or maybe he just preferred to be at home for the weekend. Either way he was most insistent and, consequently, he and Dad were allowed to go home, as long as they returned to the hospital on Monday – the day before the procedure would take place. Ironically, it turned out that the nurses were rather over-egging the pudding by warning George against using a laptop, even while wearing dark glasses. This was to make George super cautious when he got home.

After receiving assurances that they could keep their allocated room and leave their non-valuable belongings in it, Dad arranged for a taxi to bring him and George home. The taxi would wait by the entrance of the new, glass hospital building and they made their way down to meet it. In order to protect himself from the light, George was covered from head to toe – with a black balaclava, sunglasses, black gloves, black tracksuit bottoms, trainers and a grey hoodie. Dad was worried the taxi driver would think he was a terrorist. Fortunately, the driver seemed somewhat unphased by the appearance of this strange apparition. Perhaps he had picked up PDT patients on previous occasions, or maybe he was just too embarrassed to ask. Either way, he greeted them briefly, drove off without comment and the journey home passed uneventfully.

When George arrived home, he went straight to

his room, drawing the curtains to keep out the sunlight and removing only his balaclava and gloves. He was reluctant to lose the sunglasses, in case he damaged his eyes. Mum and Dad tried to persuade him that he was being a little over-cautious, but he wasn't to be moved. He was obviously worried and they decided to let him be. And so, he settled down on his bed to listen to music or text on his phone. For the next few days he kept to his room, only coming downstairs in the evening to eat in the kitchen with the lights low, or to play with the dog in the darkened hallway.

Three days later he was back at UCH for PDT treatment to his jaw. Unfortunately, he and Dad had lost their room after all, and their possessions had been moved up to a large room on another ward. They were to spend the best part of four days in this rather bare high-rise abode, sitting bored and isolated, with the lights off or down very low and the television and laptop off for the first two days, spending a good deal of time reading, sleeping or gazing out of the huge office-style windows, across a grey London landscape. Mostly, the vertical blinds were kept half-closed, although George's bed was away from the window, and he was only allowed this latter pleasure once the daylight had faded into dusk. Mum made the journey backwards and forwards from home and found it hard to keep awake in the semi-gloom. After a couple of days, George was informed by the consultant that he would have been absolutely fine using his laptop with sunglasses on and that he had definitely been led to be a little over-cautious. He switched some lights on and gave George a light meter, in order that he could check the light levels himself and take control of staying within safe limits.

On Tuesday, the PDT procedure went well and on Thursday evening the patient returned home, covered from head to toe once again, but this time picked up by Buppou. He posted on Facebook the next day:

"operation/procedure thing went well yesterday, although he thinks he might have offended one of the anaesthetists with one of his sarcastic comments :L. she goes to me: "hi im .... one of the anaesthetists" so i replied, "hi im george, im the patient" and like all her colleagues laughed and she was bare embarrassed. Im surprised she didnt shank me whilst i was asleep lol"

On the evening of the day of the operation George was in a hurry to get home because it was prize giving at his old school and he was determined to go. He had been nominated for a prize. The prize in question was a special award, given every year to one pupil from each educational key stage, for 'Endeavour leading to Achievement'. Well, that was certainly George, who had worked hard – given the stress, the bouts of feeling unwell and the endless distractions, not to mention his increasing absence from school. To study for exams with a 'chemo brain' was not an easy thing to do. Everyone in the family was proud of him.

---o---

Mum, Dad, Louis and George arrived at the all-boys school when the hall was already packed with pupils and parents. They seated themselves half-way down on the right, behind a double row of other boys who had been in Year 11 with George. He greeted his best friends and some other mates in that minimalist style of teenage boys and presently the ceremony started. The head teacher gave an address and the prize giving itself began, interspersed with a number of short speeches and some musical interludes, during which various pupils performed. Finally it was the turn of the past Year 11 boys to queue up and file on to the stage one by one to collect their prizes, before returning to their seats in front of Mum and Dad. George's prize was announced last, the head teacher declaring that he had no hesitation in choosing who should receive the special 'John Enstone Award for Endeavour leading to Achievement'.

What happened next took Mum, Dad and Louis completely by surprise, when suddenly, as George's name was called out and he moved up on to the stage (having dared to remove his hood for a few minutes in the low-level, artificial light), the two rows of boys in front of Mum and Dad arose as one to give him a standing ovation. The rest of the audience looked on in amazement. The tears welled in Mum, Dad and Louis's eyes but, George being George, he simply smiled to himself, took his prize and made his way coolly back to his seat. Later that evening he posted on Facebook:

"says thanks to all you southborough lads who helped me thru last year and especially to those who gave me standing ovation at prize giving tday :)"

---o---

After the prize giving, the rest of the autumn passed without major incident. George suffered some pain and soreness in his jaw, some stiffness in his knee and a bit of a reaction to a swine flu jab. The light sensitivity from the PDT wore off pretty quickly and the new chemotherapy continued to be reasonably tolerated. However, by December, George's mouth was becoming increasingly sore and ulcerated. He was assured it was not a side-effect of the PDT, but no one seemed completely sure whether it was caused by the chemotherapy.

Meanwhile, things at the new school were not going well. George had managed to attend for the first two weeks, during an extended induction period, when he had started to build many potential friendships. Then, after two weeks, the pupils were split into their subject groups. Unfortunately for George, many of his new friends were not taking his subjects. To make things worse, he was then absent for a good deal of the autumn term for the PDT and various other hospital appointments, consequently missing out on a bonding period in the new groups.

As time went on, it seemed to his parents that George became a face at school that everyone recognised, but no one really knew him. He seemed to chat with other students briefly in classes and amuse them with his sharp wit, but outside lessons there appeared to be no real friendships developing. Mum and Dad were also becoming increasingly concerned about the way the new school was handling things, appearing as it did at times to be little more than an exam factory. Although teachers made promises, they didn't seem able to keep them, whether through lack of time, experience or inclination.

His old school, which had boasted an excellent pastoral support department, seemed to have genuinely invested in George's well being. At the new school, he was unknown and, as a sixth-former, was expected to have a certain degree of autonomy. But George needed support and Mum, Dad and Despina began to wonder if it wouldn't be better for him to return to his former school. George, however, was not interested. He had made his move and wanted to succeed in his plans. It was as if returning to his previous school would have been a step backwards, an admission of failure. And once George had set his mind to something he was not to be easily dissuaded. Unfortunately, the situation at the school didn't improve as the year progressed.

During this period, Louis had also been looking at new schools. The following year he would move on to secondary school – a big step for any kid, but even bigger for a boy whose brother has cancer. Every move forward, every activity in his life had the potential to trip him up, to present difficulties to be overcome in relation to cancer in the family. What if he had to have time off school? Who should he tell about George's cancer? What if he was feeling bad? What if he couldn't go to someone's party, or had to be back early to go to the hospital? Mum knew cancer in the family was all encompassing; it let no one off. But it had to be managed; family life had to continue – and they all made an effort to ensure it did.

Louis had his own views on the subject of schools. He expressed an interest in going to George's old school. He had been attracted by the local state boys' grammar school at first, but he wasn't sure if he'd really fit in, with all the Justin Bieber haircuts and the silly capes worn in the sixth form. His dad came from the estates in Brixton and his mum was a working class Essex girl, born in North London. And at his brother's old school, the staff and older pupils knew George and knew the family situation. Louis said he wanted to be at a school where the support would be there "if things get bad." The open evening had been really great and he was definitely impressed by the pastoral support on offer. At the grammar school they didn't even seem to know what the word meant.

"So much for superior intelligence," thought Louis.

Yes, he knew what he needed and he would choose accordingly. He would sit the entrance test for the grammar school and would like to get in, but secretly he was drawn to his brother's old school. In the meantime, there were SATS to prepare for. And all the while he was fast outgrowing his old school, along with many of his mates.

Meanwhile, the autumn term came to an end and Christmas was here once again. The tree went up, mince pies were baked, presents were wrapped and on Christmas Eve Dad received a phone call on his mobile – from UCH. There was good news at last. Apparently, the latest scans suggested that the PDT treatment was working.

The consultant's exact words were, "I am cautiously optimistic."

It was the best present of all and delivered just in time for Christmas! There was joy throughout the family.

That year, on Christmas Day, they all sat once again – Mum, Dad, George, Despina and Louis – drinking champagne before dinner and discussing the year to come. Yiayia and Buppou had been invited too. They all remained hopeful, but it was hard to believe that a whole year had passed since the five of them had gathered for the same discussion last Christmas. The situation was now much worse, but they remained as optimistic as they could, especially given the news from UCH.

After Christmas, there followed five days in Southwold as usual, for Mum, Dad and the boys – a second Christmas lunch and presents with Nanny Olive in the flat by the sea. This year Mum and Dad had found the perfect hat for Nanny Olive to buy George (she wasn't up to Christmas shopping any more, and so she always asked Mum and Dad to purchase her presents for the boys). It was one of those woollen hats in fashion at the time, with a long plait hanging down on either side. It was pink and grey striped and George loved it, especially as pink was 'in' for boys that year. From then on, he would mostly be seen wearing it everywhere.

On one of the days in Southwold, friends who owned a holiday cottage nearby came to visit them and they had a good time, despite their underlying fears. Emma was an old friend of Mum's, and the latter was always happy to see her, her husband and their three children. Their eldest daughter was just a few months younger than George. A couple of years previously Mum, Dad and the boys had visited them in their 'cottage', which had turned out to be quite large and had two staircases that the children spent their time running up and down, playing hide-and-seek – George's favourite game of course. At one point, George and the oldest girl had hidden in a double wardrobe. When Louis had opened one door to look inside, they had sneakily crept out of the other and run off to find a new hiding place. There was generally a lot of laughter and running around. Now, however, George was quiet and Mum and Dad were conscious of how difficult it was for him; his face was swollen and he looked pale and thin compared to the friends' healthy teenage girl. But he remained present during tea and cake, if somewhat subdued.

After that, New Year passed in Southwold, with glasses of champagne again and a nice meal in the flat. In all of them there existed simultaneously both a sense of apprehension and a cautious optimism. They endured the difficult times and engaged with the good things in life as best they could. They had once again seen the old year out with cancer amongst them; now it was time to return home to see what the new one would bring.

For The Love of George

11. Insomnia and the Ash Cloud

Another year had begun and it started in style for George. At the end of the first week in January, Louis, Dad and Mum accompanied him to Mercedes Benz World. Mum and Dad had purchased an off-road driving experience for George for Christmas; the rest of them were to go along as passengers.

They arrived at the large glass building that was Mercedes Benz World just after lunch and spent an hour looking around the museum, which they all found quite interesting. Mum admired the old sports convertibles, while George and Louis, great fans of 'Top Gear', were much more taken with the latest models. They climbed in and out of the new cars, sat behind the steering wheels, imagining themselves the proud owners and discussed the technical details with Dad. Then the four of them went down to rendezvous with the instructor for George's lesson.

After some initial discussion the instructor led them outside to their car. George followed confidently, hoisting up his typically low-slung jeans as he went, and adjusting his favourite bling around his neck. He slipped quickly into the driver's seat, keen to get going with his first-ever driving experience. Learning to drive the vehicle was simple, as the car was automatic and had dual controls, meaning George mainly had to steer and control two pedals. He was a quick learner and was soon setting off confidently on the course. The instructor started him off gently, but before long he had progressed to the more interesting aspects of the course that he had been looking forward to. From then on, he gleaned a great deal of pleasure from climbing short, steep slopes, bumping down the other side, speeding along gullies at a forty-five degree angle that made Mum think the car would turn over and generally tearing around as if he was on some long-distance rally. At one point he was asked to reverse up and over an almost vertical, bumpy mound, prompting a certain amount of suppressed squealing from one of the passengers. They all enjoyed themselves greatly and George was well pleased with his present. It was good to see him taking control and engaging with something so enthusiastically.

A photo posted on Facebook in January showed George and two mates – George looking intently at the camera with his clear brown eyes, his head shaved, a wry smile just dancing at the edges of his mouth and eyes, his thumb and forefinger of his right hand spread apart to support his prominent chin. It was George with his mates, George looking confident and cool.

In the weeks following the driving experience,

George continued with his chemotherapy and new scans were performed. A bone scan showed 'hot spots' on the jaw and on the pelvis. Dad spoke to Mr Hyde and he agreed that it was possible those on the pelvis were a result of trauma, due to mechanical change in the area -— that is, from a change of gait after the first operation, when bone had been taken from the hip. Alison at the Marsden was not convinced and the possibility of metastases to the pelvis was added to the diagnosis.

Ironically, the area of concern on the knee was now being disputed by various experts. It seemed that it probably wasn't tumour after all. Mum and Dad wished they'd never taken George to the Marsden when the knee had swollen up. Perhaps then he would have had his second operation on the jaw and they would be in a better place by now. Meanwhile, the 'hot spot' on the pelvis – at the sacroiliac joint – was the latest cause for concern. If it turned out to be tumour, then things were worse than they had feared.

---o---

At the beginning of February George had his second round of PDT. Unfortunately, this time there was a delay of several hours and it wasn't until early evening that he was finally taken down for surgery. He had been starved all day and was getting bored and frustrated by the wait. Everyone was feeling strained, not knowing exactly why there was such a delay, and Mum was distressed at having to leave the hospital before he went down, in order to get back home for Louis. After the procedure George spent another ten days retreating from the light, although a little less cautiously this time round. Then there followed a period of great discomfort.

George began to suffer a number of side-effects, almost certainly caused by the chemotherapy. The worst was an unbearable burning and itching, especially at night. Consequently, he was unable to get a proper night's sleep and although he was prescribed various anti-histamines, these had little effect. Eventually, he began going in late to school or missing whole days from sheer exhaustion. As a result, the isolation at school worsened and fatigue meant he found it increasingly difficult to apply himself to schoolwork at home.

One day he was sitting in Costa Coffee with Despina, spending time leafing through cookbooks and travel books – brother and big sister, temporarily lost in another world, happy for a moment in their friendship, leaving troubles behind. They munched their mini muffins and sipped their coffee, discussing all the things they would love to eat and the places they would travel to if they could. But then George began to talk about school. He described how miserable he was there and how he would sometimes 'bunk off' and just go and sit alone in Costa and read. It was an upsetting picture that he painted. Dad hoped it was not quite as bad as this. Later on, he found that George had spent time with some girls from school and he wondered whether some of the time was spent drinking coffee with them, but they would never know. There were certainly things he wouldn't tell Mum and Dad.

Then he contracted a couple of viruses, which

resulted in admission to the local hospital. Following this, he developed a rash on his chest, back and face, and his mouth became inflamed again.

In the end, everyone was becoming strung out with the disturbed nights. George tried his best to deal with the itching and burning; rising from bed at around 1.00 a.m. and pacing his room until he could bear it no longer and had to knock on his parents' door for help. Mostly Dad would get up and try to calm him down, returning to bed exhausted after an hour and a half, drifting into a fitful sleep before rising early to set off for work. Then they discovered that plunging George's feet in a bowl of ice-cold water containing lavender oil helped a little and this became a ritual that he indulged in every night. He also wrote about his experience, viewing himself in the third person carrying out these nightly rituals, analysing all the little details of what was occurring to him physically, perhaps in a bid to keep his sanity. Mum and Dad read his account:

Up all night

He flung his eyes open at long last. Having awoken some time previously, he had tried denying it was anything to do with the subject that had occupied and dominated his life for over a month now. He promised himself it was merely psychological and that having suspected that what had now occurred would occur, it had become a self fulfilling prophecy. Dragging his legs round to the edge of his bed, he dropped them over the side and pulled with a grunt his now severely thin torso up into a sitting position. Pausing momentarily to yawn and wipe any last remains of sleep from within his dark, hazel eyes, he drew himself to his full height. Dragging his feet lazily across his fading bedroom floor with a soft rustle accompanying each step, he made his way to his rather rickety desk and took a seat calmly upon the swivel chair that stood beside it.

The excruciating burning sensation in his hands and feet was now at his full attention, however as his father had informed him many a time, he stayed as calm as possible so as not to provoke the situation any further. Peering through the darkness he was surprised that he could not see a faint red glow from either his hands or feet, as he was sure they were of a sufficient temperature to produce such a thing as a by-product of the reaction happening beneath his very skin.

He imagined what it may look like at microscopic detail, possibly little explosions as cells reacted fiercely with one another, creating tiny pricks of light and of course, high concentrations of heat. Enough to have taken him to the edge of insanity increasingly more frequently than he and indeed his parents were comfortable with.

Blinking, he returned back to Earth, back to his bedroom. One of three in a household of four people. His sister, having moved out many years previously, had vacated this very room for him in the process and so, he gladly took up the opportunity to gather his belongings in the room he had shared with his brother and set up for an unmistakeably quieter life on his own.

Arranging his thoughts carefully and focusing much of his will power on keeping his temper low and breathing steady he began the process he had practised the night before.

Rolling his pyjama bottoms up to his knees he prepared himself for what he knew would be an experience he didn't care much for. Throwing his eyes open wide and opening his mouth to its fullest he managed, only just, to suppress a cry of shock. Never had he felt such a contrast in sensation. From the burning, tortuously irritating sensation that had brought him to this very time and place, the bowl of water he had just plunged his punished feet into was of another world. Having tried swimming in the North Sea on holiday in Suffolk and thought it cold, the small bowl of water his feet were now immersed in could well have come from the Arctic and most certainly out did the North Sea, which in comparison was welcomingly warm. The liquid, soft and aromatic from him having added Lavender oil, lapped at his feet. Swirling and engulfing its two sorry victims, the fold of the disturbed water wrapped itself around his ankles. The icy liquid, serpent like in its actions began to slow all movement, calming again as it sucked the hot, fiery innards from its now conquered prey.

As he became accustomed to the temperature, George, although he didn't like to admit it, was under the impression that the experience was becoming likeable. Refreshing.

Squeezing at the side of his phone, he pressed a button, causing the back light for the front of his mobile

*phone to pop into life. The time read 00:57 in thick,
almost condemning black digital numbers. Like
clockwork he thought, as he cast his mind back to the
previous nights that week, knowing every other time he
had been woken by his body's severely damaged internal
clock was around the same. All of them around twelve,
leaning towards one o'clock in some cases, much like the
events unfolding at the present time.*

*Having decided the not too masculine process of
giving his feet a nice soak in essential oils had gone on
long enough, he removed them and placed them within
the soft, cotton folds of his towel. It lay prearranged,
neatly on the floor next to the bowl he had just removed
his feet from. Remembering the instructions he had seen
many a time whilst researching helpful remedies of such
a problem as the one he was witnessing daily, he
proceeded to pat, rather than rub, his feet dry. He was
certain that his dad had also warned against the ill idea
of rubbing due to the fact that the process would release
hormones, which would in turn do no good to the
situation. Provoke it more than anything. Rather than
racking his brain for the name of such hormones, he
finished up drying his left foot and moved on to the right,
being extremely thorough between the toes as he didn't
welcome the idea of having a fungal infection such as
athletes foot in addition to the ailments he already
possessed.*

*Raising himself up, he rested his back against the
cushioned back support of the chair and marvelled at the
refreshed feeling that now enthralled his feet. Smiling to*

himself and almost chuckling at the notion that he may have just found a short term fix to a problem that had begun to spiral an unimaginable amount out of control. As he now thought about it, the idea was such a simple one that it was madness, the fact that neither he nor his extremely knowledgeable parents had thought of it. Perhaps that very reason was why. The fact that the idea be so simple, it was possible it was overlooked for the mere reason it seemed TOO simple and therefore out of the league of the complicated, yet delicate processes and functions of the human body. As he had said many a time to his parents, George truly believed that despite its amazing capabilities and mind bogglingly complex systems and sub systems and micro systems, the human body could be (in some cases) an increasingly flawed organism. Being known to attack itself, to throw itself into vicious circles and downward spirals whereby the body's reaction to a problem can cause the individual to make said problem worse by reacting to it in ways that seem to come naturally. But then again it's what defines what we are as human beings, as the most developed animals on the planet.

Mum, Dad, Despina, Louis and the rest of the family read this account; it was impossible not to be moved by the experience of one so young struggling to deal with the irritating, and sometimes unbearable symptoms that plagued him and to make sense of the runaway events that were taking over his life. They were impressed by his ability to capture the experience in written word. It was so different from the George who rarely communicated his thoughts and feelings verbally. And it seemed to capture perfectly that strange and lonely world of the insomniac.

There were some nights when Mum couldn't sleep either – she was also something of an insomniac and would be up in the night, maybe two or three times a week. She would go downstairs to make a cup of tea and if the light were off in George's room, would breathe a sigh of relief, thinking he must be asleep for once. But, on descending the stairs, she would often spy him lying in the hall in his thin, navy blue dressing gown, curled up foetus-like with Flash for comfort. Invariably he would fall asleep, and there they would lay, dog and master curled up in perfect harmony. Mum would disturb the harmony by sending George back up to bed, worrying that he would catch cold in the draughty hallway. She should have sent Flash up with him, but her mania for keeping some areas of the house free from dog hairs overruled her heart. Besides, George had tried having Flash sleep in his room when they had first brought him home and it hadn't gone well. George had complained that the dog moved about restlessly and kept him awake, prompting the parents to move Flash downstairs on a permanent basis. Once this was done, Mum was reluctant to go back on it. However, during one particularly bad night of insomnia, she found boy and dog asleep together in George's bed.

In the mornings, it was Mum's duty to rouse George and she would attempt to get him out of bed by

10.30, in order that his sleep patterns wouldn't become irreversibly disturbed. She knew the situation could worsen, as tumour cells never sleep, working away 24 hours a day, sucking up glucose, protecting their environment, growing new blood vessels and dividing and proliferating constantly. Eventually the enforced rising – 'sleep hygiene' the psychologists called it – and the prescription of melatonin (the chemical produced naturally by the body to alert us that it is time to sleep) had some positive effect. But it was a cruel thing to have to do, to goad an exhausted child into wakefulness and send him off to school looking sickly, pale and worn out. Mum and Dad were still keen that George should focus on having a future, that he shouldn't give up on school because somehow that seemed like giving up on life. Sometimes their efforts to steer him away from thinking about the possibility of death were bordering on obsession.

George was struggling at school, but as ever, he made light of it to his mates on Facebook:

"any one know what time psychology revision is tommorow? knew i shud have paid attention in class when the teachers were talkin bout it lol."

Instead, he focused on other interests that he had in common with his friends: "clash of the titans 3D is tooo sikk!"

At one point, in despair, Mum and Dad took George to a hypnotherapist, but he found it difficult to engage with this method. Instead, he began to visit the counsellor at the Marsden and this seemed to provide some support for him. Dad also began to make appointments to see her, to deal with his increasing fear that his son was going to die. She once observed that he was already in mourning while his son was still alive. Within a year Mum and Despina had also attended appointments.

Finally, at the end of six weeks, a decision was made to stop the chemotherapy – a decision that George was instrumental in, as he could no longer endure the side effects. Then, to make things worse, a new MRI scan produced an unclear picture of what was happening in his jaw. By April, however, it was clear that the PDT had not been successful, at which point George became unreasonably angry with himself for not enduring the chemotherapy because he now had no treatment and the tumour was growing.

After that everything seemed to grind to a halt, with no further treatments being proffered by the Marsden and they seemed to be up a blind alley going nowhere. In a phone call to Dad, Alison explained that the disease was no longer curable. Mum and Dad requested a meeting with her during which they asked her not to communicate this information to George, as they were concerned his condition would deteriorate rapidly with such knowledge, and they still wished to explore other treatments. She complied, although the incurability of his disease was still implied in the discussions she had with George, and Mum and Dad never really knew how much of this he understood.

They didn't hear from UCH again; there was no

contact to discuss the outcome of the PDT or any response to Dad's emails. Consequently, they were unable to form a clear picture of what had happened. The PDT consultant cut off all contact, placing everything in the hands of Alison at the Marsden and leaving the family with no feeling of closure. It felt as if they had never existed for him, as if there was a deliberate blanking of George now that it was clear the treatment had been unsuccessful. Mum, Dad and George were angry and upset. After all, a little humanity goes a long way.

His parents tried to reassure George that there were still other options to explore, but in reality they were struggling to know where to turn. When they received the news that Alison was leaving and would be replaced with someone less experienced, they began to feel as if they had been cut adrift. They could see themselves floating slowly away from their moorings, with no one hearing their cries for help. Mum and Dad racked their brains.

They wondered if Mr Hyde could help. Since he regarded the hotspot on the pelvis as feasibly mechanical rather than tumour, and since the knee hadn't shown any signs of developing into anything – and in fact may have been a complete red herring – perhaps now he would consider operating on the jaw again? It was a long shot, but what did they have to lose? They decided to make contact directly with Mr Hyde. Dad emailed him and they waited for a response.

Around this time the results of the entrance tests for the boy's grammar school came in. Approximately 1400 boys from far and wide had taken the test and no single boy from Louis's school had been offered a place, which surprised everyone. Louis was both disappointed and relieved at the same time. Fortunately he had also applied to his brother's old school and in March was informed that he had been accepted. George said it was a good choice and Louis became very excited about the prospect of starting there; in fact he couldn't wait.

Meanwhile, Dad had been in touch with an oncologist in Frankfurt, who specialised in radio-frequency ablation – a therapy that involved surgical destruction of tissue using radio waves. After studying the scans Dad had sent him, he informed them he was prepared to treat George, and although the NHS was not prepared to pay for the treatment, Mum and Dad decided to proceed. Luckily they had funds that had been invested for the children from life insurance when George and Despina's mum had died and it seemed appropriate that some of this should go towards trying to save George. They were only too aware that this was not an option open to many families.

And so George and Dad began preparing for a trip to Germany. Mum schooled them in a few basic German phrases, learnt at O level many years before. She wondered if she had set them up to look like complete muppets, but then she knew languages were not Dad's strong point anyway. Dad had been to Frankfurt before on business, but was looking forward to actually seeing something of the city this time.

---o---

On Wednesday 14th April 2010 George and Dad

set off for Frankfurt. They hadn't looked at the news that morning and were not aware they were about to take the last flight out of Heathrow Airport before the Icelandic ash cloud closed down European airspace. The only inkling they had as they approached the airport that something was perhaps amiss was from the distinct lack of planes taking off, which caused them to wonder if there was some kind of security alert. As they entered the departure lounge, the boards were flashing red with cancellations and they began to worry that their own flight would be cancelled. It was only after take-off, when they had settled themselves down for the duration of the flight, that they saw the headlines in the newspapers and realised the scale of the event. They were somewhat relieved to have got away before everything was shut down.

Back home, Mum and Louis were left alone for a few days. Louis went to school, while Mum put the finishing touches to the final draft of her thesis. They walked the dog, watched a film or two together and tried to look after each other. Flash was a comfort when Dad and George were away. Every night, before going to bed, Mum would sit him down, give him his milky biscuits and tell him to look after her and Louis. He would gaze at her intently, ears pricked up, as if he knew she was saying something important. Then he'd roll on to his back, legs in the air, to get his goodnight tummy rub!

Several hundred miles away in Frankfurt, George and Dad settled into their hotel – a modest, white building on the edge of a roundabout leading onto a bridge across the river. Their room was pretty spartan, with two single beds, a toilet/bathroom and a desk and chair. Although not exactly uncomfortable, it was clearly designed primarily for business visitors. The hotel was situated about five minutes walk from the main station in one direction and from the largest European financial centre outside London in the other. Approaching the area in the taxi from the airport, George was impressed by the sight of the numerous skyscrapers looming up ahead. The hotel was also not far from Frankfurt University Hospital on the other side of the river, where George would be treated.

On the afternoon of their arrival, after resting a while, they set off to explore a little. They browsed in the shops, wandered along the river and generally imbibed the local atmosphere. George was amused in one shop to spot a magazine entitled 'Bum'. He was disappointed however when a closer look revealed a glossy TV mag full of information on celebrities – nothing to do with the more promising subject suggested by the English translation of the title. After that, they explored the train station where there was a general buzz created by the shops and cafés, which made it a pleasant place to tarry over the coming days.

That first evening they ate an Indian meal, ordering a nominally much hotter curry than they would normally have risked, allowing for the milder German palate, which was unused to the caustic levels of heat available in UK curry houses. In the next few days, they would investigate several of the little eateries because

George was keen to try everything – including the many different types of pork and endless varieties of pickled cabbage, as well as the food on offer in the Chinese restaurants. Food came to dominate their stay somewhat, as it was a constant struggle to find types of cuisine that were not dominated by meat or high carbohydrate foods, both of which Dad was keen to limit George's consumption. Consequently, no sooner had they started on their lunch each day than they were discussing where to have dinner.

George, keen to explore the city at street level rather than through tourist attractions, was intrigued by everything. He was like a child drinking in new experiences and it dawned on Dad that his son had never been to a big city outside London; Mum and Dad had always tended towards taking quiet holidays in the country or by the sea. Now George was fascinated by the goings on in this different world – the big German cars, the huge array of pork products set out for breakfast at the hotel, the comings and goings at the station. He was far more of a city boy, interested in machines and technology, as well as those small, material differences that help define a culture.

On their second day, they set off on foot to cross the bridge over the river and walk to the hospital, where they would keep their first appointment with the consultant. As they entered the large hospital building they were struck by the contrast with their National Health Service (NHS) experiences back home. Frankfurt University Hospital was modern, clean and above all calm. Although they were still to experience some considerable waiting around during their first visit, they both agreed that it was far more pleasant to do so in the calm atmosphere and soothing environment that contrasted so sharply with the crowded, hectic and depressing surroundings in the London hospitals that George had attended.

They met their consultant, a tall, rather severe-looking man, who dressed in a white lab coat and spent more time staring at scans and his computer than he did looking people in the eye. He was cool and distant and George didn't really warm to him, although there was nothing exactly bad about him. He was clearly a very busy man and they noticed that this gave him an air of distraction too. Whilst Dad found him willing to enter into discussion, he wondered what the reaction would have been if they had disagreed with his proposals, as he seemed like a man who, once he had made up his mind, was not to be moved.

First of all, an MRI scan of George's jaw was carried out, in order to have the latest images to work from. Afterwards, they waited around for the results, which produced a disappointing outcome. The consultant didn't consider, after all, that radio frequency ablation to the jaw was feasible. The new MRI showed that there had been disease progression, even since the scan at the Marsden. It was a shock and Dad, tense and worried most of the time, wondered how fast the tumour was growing. George, as usual, was laid back and actually becoming pretty bored with all the hanging around. He spent his time focused on his iPod and listening to music. In the end, the consultant recommended instead a treatment called chemo-perfusion, which George agreed to have and they returned the next day for this purpose.

As it would turn out, the procedure for chemo-perfusion unnerved George more than most of the treatments he underwent in the whole period of his cancer. It involved threading a fine line into the groin and up through his body in order to inject a chemotherapy drug directly into the tumour. To say it was not a pleasant experience for him was an understatement. As the line passed up through George's body, the consultant was studying its progress on a monitor, to avoid any deviation from the chosen route. It was necessary for the patient to be awake, in order that he could be asked to hold his breath as the doctor navigated around the heart, and so George was only lightly sedated. Occasionally the line would hit a nerve causing George's arms to fly out involuntarily. This lack of control frightened him considerably and the consultant was finally unable to complete all of the treatment. It was upsetting for Dad to see George in such distress, and, in addition, Dad wasn't too hopeful about the outcome of the procedure. George was just relieved it didn't have to be repeated. After it was over, in true George style, he went off to sleep for hours much to Dad's frustration.

Once the chemo-perfusion was over, they assumed they would have just one free day before the flight home. They had kept a wary eye on the events surrounding the ash cloud, hoping it would pass by the time they were due to return to England, but now it was not looking good. Although by the end of treatment they had been in Frankfurt for three days, it would be a further four days before they were home. Meanwhile, their small hotel filled to bursting with frustrated, bored tourists, including a large contingent of Chinese people, who could be seen constantly searching the Internet for information on potential routes home. Dad and George had nothing to do but keep an eye on the news, wander Frankfurt aimlessly or sit in their tiny hotel room. The long, tedious days were getting them down, when one evening they were somewhat enlivened by witnessing a near-riot at the station.

It was late and they were just taking a short stroll after dinner, before returning to their hotel. As they came to the railway station, there were suddenly flashing lights and the sound of sirens all around, followed by the appearance of dozens of military police running into the station. Curious to see what had provoked such a display, Dad and George followed them and were amazed to see the station concourse full of opposing groups of football supporters. With their painted faces and team scarves, they were noisily facing up to each other for a fight. The police were now struggling to keep them apart, joining arms and separating small groups to prevent the fight from kicking off. George, who showed no signs of fear or nervousness, was fascinated and keen to get in close to observe. To him, it was like watching some virtual reality TV programme – nothing to do with him, but something interesting to talk about when he got home. He edged as close as Dad would allow him, but in the final event, was disappointed, as nothing much happened; a few fans were arrested, trains arrived and the rest of the troublemakers dispersed. Dad and George were back to the reality of boredom and waiting.

As they wandered the streets during those few days, one of the most worrying things was the increasing pain in the pelvis suffered by George. It was becoming evident that the problem at the sacroiliac joint was not going to go away. The delights of Frankfurt had completely worn off and all father and son wanted to do was get back home. However, this was proving considerably harder than they had hoped. George was not impressed, as was clear from his Facebook posting:

"stuck in Germany and not sure when he'll be allowed out :@. Fucking Volcano sneezing all over the place"

Despite the controversy and the endless wrangling between the airway companies and the UK government, there were no flights home. European airspace was mostly still closed in the face of considerable opposition from the public, as well as many aviation experts. Along with thousands of others, Dad and George were therefore stranded and forced to investigate alternative routes for getting back. Unfortunately, even here they drew a blank because unsurprisingly everyone else had the same idea and the UK government was less than useless in coming to the aid of its stranded citizens. Eventually, it was the company Dad worked for who saved the day, finding them a passage on a ferry from Caen to Portsmouth, via German and French railways.

---o---

It was a weekday evening when Mum and Louis packed Flash into the car and set off for Portsmouth harbour, where the ferry was due to dock at around 8.30. The car journey was uneventful until they were just five minutes away from the ferry terminal, at which point they spent half an hour driving round and round the same huge complex of roundabouts, trying to find the correct road. The signs were unclear and they made the same mistake three times. When Mum was almost on the point of despair, they pulled into a service station and obtained directions from the cashier. This time they successfully negotiated the convoluted jumble of roads and finally arrived at the ferry port, somewhat tired, but otherwise none the worse for wear. A few months later Mum and Dad overheard a conversation in a restaurant about the difficulties of finding your way around Portsmouth. Mum felt vindicated.

The ferry terminal was extremely busy. The arrivals building was packed and unfortunately dogs were not allowed in. Luckily, Mum and Louis found an empty spot to sit with Flash – on the floor, just inside the automatic doors – hoping that some concession would be made if they kept him under control. As usual the dog attracted a great many "ooh"s and "ah"s from passers by. He was handsome and cute and lapped up every bit of attention.

They were becoming bored and a little anxious, when finally at 10 p.m. the weary travellers appeared. They had docked more than an hour previously, but had been kept squashed into a corridor on board waiting to disembark, putting a good deal of strain on George's hip and on Dad's nerves. Apparently, foot passengers were not allowed to walk the 100 metres to the terminal buildings and, with the ferries packed to bursting, there was a long wait while the small number of ferrying vehicles worked their way through the queue. The two travellers were frustrated and exhausted, but happy to see Mum and Louis and surprised to see Flash. They piled into the car for the long drive home and, at last, by 1.00 a.m. they were all back home and tucked up safely in bed. George's Facebook posting read "after 20 something hours of travelling is finaly home (smiley face)."

The next day, they received the first piece of good news since Christmas, when Mr Hyde contacted Dad and informed him that a new operation was possible. Having studied the latest scans he was prepared to go ahead, in view of the lack of development in the sites at the hip and knee. There was great rejoicing and they made an appointment to see him the following week. Meanwhile, they had an appointment with George's new consultant oncologist, and to this end, they set off late one morning to make the now all-too-familiar journey to the Marsden.

---o---

At Day Care in the Children's Unit, they were subjected to the usual long wait to see a consultant. All three of them buried their heads in their books, in a desperate attempt to avoid the resident clown entertainers, who always seemed unable to differentiate between five and fifteen year olds. At last George's name was called and they went to sit outside the consultant's door, waiting to be asked in.

When they entered, they saw that the new consultant was a heavy-set woman in early middle age. She wore plain, sensible clothes and shoes and had a rather mumbling, serious, academic style. She appeared to be still finding her feet in her new role and determined to play things by the book. Unfortunately, George, Dad and Mum were not drawn to her. And from that moment, they entered into a long wrangle with her.

Dad had been in touch with another German consultant, who treated cancer patients with a metronomic therapy. His protocol involved taking a daily, oral, low-dose chemotherapy, along with other drugs such as celecoxib (an anti-inflammatory painkiller), the aim being to destroy the conditions required for a tumour to thrive. The additional drugs were already in use for the treatment of other conditions, such as diabetes. Mum and Dad were confident that the treatment would be supported by the Marsden, as there was nothing controversial about the particular drugs, except that they hadn't been tried in this combination in the UK for the treatment of cancer. The German consultant offered to be an advisor, albeit via email and telephone. Their new consultant oncologist remained unconvinced, stalled on giving an answer to the family and eventually refused on the basis that this protocol was experimental and no one at the Marsden had experience of using it. Mum and Dad were furious, especially as initially nothing was offered to George in its place.

Meanwhile, Mr Hyde explained the procedure for the new operation. Mum and Dad wondered what would have happened if they hadn't taken the initiative and contacted him. Would George have been offered anything? They wondered what late-stage cancer patients were expected to do? Just give up and prepare to die quietly? Later on, they would hear stories from other cancer patients in the UK, suggesting this was exactly what was expected.

Mr Hyde explained that, as planned for the previously cancelled operation, bone for the reconstruction would be taken from George's fibula. The first jaw reconstruction would need to be removed, plus a little extra – down to the middle of the chin. He would be admitted to St Anthony's private hospital for the operation to take place a little over a week later, on Saturday 15th May 2010. At last they had a new plan, and one that offered new hope. Accordingly, they began to make preparations

For The Love of George

12. Fighting for His Life

St Anthony's Hospital was notably different to St George's – very small by comparison and more like a hotel than a hospital. It was set in pleasant grounds, with benches placed amongst the lawns and flowerbeds. The individual, en-suite rooms were well-equipped, carpeted and quiet. The elderly matron, who headed the establishment, was also the mother superior of the adjacent convent, and patient-centred care appeared to be a reality: nurses seemed to have time to be attentive to patients. Even the small canteen made an effort to transcend the usual hospital fare, albeit not always successfully. The family was impressed. So this was what private health care meant. It was like travelling first class for the first time and seeing how the other half lives. Thank goodness they had private health insurance to cover it because they weren't sure how George would have coped with another stay at St George's.

After booking in, they were taken up to a small ward on the first floor, where George's room looked out over the car park and grassy area at the front of the hospital. Having tried out the remote control for the bed and tested it to its limits, George grabbed the TV remote and settled down to a spot of television, while Mum did her usual – tidying away all the bags left lying around by George and Dad. Later on, Mr Hyde paid a visit to check everything was ok. George posted on Facebook:

"up at 7:00 tommorow for a 10ish hour operation, just how I love to spend my weekends :L."

Surgery was set for the morning of Saturday 15th May and George went down to theatre early. It was another long day and Mum and Dad passed the time as they had during the first operation at St George's. Rules were a little more stringent at St Anthony's and for one awful moment they thought they wouldn't be allowed into the pre-op room to see George go under. However, concessions were made and George, his usual jokey self, was soon slipping away into that helpless state of anaesthetic sleep. He really was amazing the way he handled everything, with no fuss at all. Even Mr Hyde had remarked that he was more mature than many of his adult patients. And so, for the second time, Mum and Dad left their son in Mr Hyde's good hands.

Mum and Dad had booked a room in the single-storey accommodation block just two minutes walk away, and they spent the morning as before – reading, dozing and answering phone calls. They had lunch in the canteen and wandered the grounds. In the afternoon, they met Buppou for a cup of tea and then went back to doze some more. After enquiring on the ward if there was any news, they ate dinner in the canteen, making enquiries again afterwards. They returned to their room and read a little, and then made their way to the ward once again at around 9.00 p.m., with a view to staying there until George was out of surgery (unlike St George's, at St Anthony's George was allowed to keep his allocated room while he was in surgery and Intensive Care). By 11.00 they were getting anxious and the sister who seemed to be the head nurse of the hospital kindly brought them a cup of tea and biscuits. They were amazed that someone so senior should be making tea for them. Finally, Mr Hyde came to see them and informed them that all had gone well, and they set off to see George, tired and full of tense anticipation at seeing him once again battered and bruised from major surgery.

They were allowed to enter the recovery ward only one at a time. Dad went in first and sat close to George, holding his hand and stroking his head, speaking gently to him and holding back the tears as best he could. Then he made way for Mum, who was by now beside herself with the tension of waiting and almost fell into the ward. She saw George's face hugely swollen and bruised, as after the first operation, and she knew it would get worse before it got better. He lay there in a drugged sleep, occasionally stirring – so much helplessness, so much hurt. Then suddenly he stirred, opened his eyes briefly – and winked at her! Well if that wasn't just George all over.

When they reached the bottom of the stairs, Mum, who rarely broke down, collapsed and sobbed, screaming silently through the sobbing. It was late at night, everywhere was quiet, empty, deserted; she was exhausted; Dad was exhausted. They went off into the cold night air and to the sparse room and single bed they would share that night.

---o---

The next day George was in Intensive Care and doing well. Despina came to visit; Yiayia and Buppou came. George's grandfather on his real mum's side made the trip from Cyprus and came to visit. He was staying with his cousin and her husband and they drove him over to see George.

Buppou Kokko was a short, stout, moustachioed man, typically Greek-Cypriot looking, who spoke a little English. Having already lost his daughter, George's mum, to cancer, he was overwhelmed by the sight of George lying helpless and swollen. In the days to come, Mum and Dad were to see him increasingly unable to deal with the situation. He seemed to want to be there but not want to be there. He would appear and sit watching George for a while and then disappear into the hospital grounds to smoke and sit alone for long periods of time. Eventually, he went back to Cyprus.

George was moved back to his room on the ward on Monday; he was glad to be there. On Tuesday he was up taking his first walk down the corridor. It was difficult for him to manoeuvre because of the removal of muscle from his back, which caused him a good deal of pain and frustration. He was still attached to a number of lines and he had a feeding tube, which would stay in for more than a week, while he watched culinary programme after programme on TV. Visitors abounded.

---o---

There was a problem. An area of skin below George's jaw was going grey. It became apparent that there was necrotic tissue, where the blood supply from the newly-hooked-up veins had not reached this area. It would be necessary for Mr Hyde to perform a skin graft and skin would be taken from George's leg, for this purpose. On Tuesday 25th May, ten days after the main operation, George was taken down for further surgery to carry out the skin graft, which was executed successfully, but now there was an additional wound – on his leg.

All this time, Mum, Despina and other visitors were travelling in and out each day; Mum would sometimes bring Louis with her. One day they brought Flash, and George hobbled down the fire escape stairs located at the end of the ward, to pat and stroke his dog. They took a short walk up to a little arbour where there were benches surrounded by lavender bushes and small trees, but George was unable to sit for long because of the pain in his back. Whilst he was recovering as expected, he was generally weak, tired and in pain. Despite this, he continued to improve a little each day, and on Wednesday of the second week he took his first proper food, on Thursday the feeding tube came out and on Friday he went home.

Now they had to wait – for the pathology results. Meanwhile, the staples from the operation were removed from his jaw, and his leg dressing was changed by the

Pediatric Outreach Nursing Team (PONT) from Kingston Hospital. The swelling to his face was still considerable and he continued to find it hard to manoeuvre.

---o---

Three weeks after returning home, they were once again in Mr Hyde's clinic at St George's, waiting to get the pathology results. Once again the news was not good: the histology showed that there was viable tumour on the bottom margin, near the chin. Fortunately, Mr Hyde could operate again in just over a week's time. And so it was that George found himself back in St Anthony's for his third major operation on his jaw, on Saturday 19th June, with Mum and Dad in tow. It was a wonder how he could keep going, but keep going he did. His Facebook post read:

"out of one operation, into another LOL. what fun times"

This time he suffered greatly. Following surgery, it was necessary to perform a tracheostomy, creating a direct opening into the trachea, to enable him to breathe, as his throat was considerably swollen. Unexpectedly, extra bone had been resected round to the left hand side of his jaw. More than half of his jaw had now been reconstructed, this time from bone in his rib, with muscle from his calf. In addition, there was another skin graft, with tissue once again taken from his leg.

The tracheostomy caused George to feel helpless and afraid. He found it difficult to use the device that was supposed to close the tube and enable the patient to voice sounds. For the first day and night in Intensive Care he was using a fingerboard to spell out each word in turn, but his large fingers moved fast and imprecisely over the letters and it was hard going for those around him to follow what he was trying to say. His post on Facebook played down the difficulties:

"managed to talk for the first time today. never get a tracheostomy whatevr you do lol"

He had his own room in Intensive Care – a large room, full of the usual equipment, but also with a number of chairs, including a recliner, which Dad slept on. The tracheostomy made it necessary for George to stay in Intensive Care for a number of days this time round. It was the only time that the family found a problem with St Anthony's.

As George was now over sixteen – one of the criteria for being admitted to the private hospital for his operation – he was treated as an adult. Therefore, strictly speaking, he wasn't allowed to have a parent to stay with him overnight. Most nurses in the intensive care unit were sympathetic, realising that George had been through a great deal, was still very young and needed his father nearby. The room was clearly large enough for Dad not to be in the way if there was an emergency. However, one particular nurse displayed a coldly clinical attitude, making it clear that as far as she was concerned the rules were made for a reason and were not to be bent. On the second evening Dad was sent packing at around midnight, leaving a distraught George at her mercy. At six o'clock Dad returned to find George in a bad way and vowed he wouldn't leave him again, no matter what. After taking his case to more senior staff, it was decided that it would be at the discretion of whoever was in charge each night, as to whether Dad was allowed to stay. Luckily he managed to avoid being sent away again, much to the relief of George and the family, but to the chagrin of the unsympathetic nurse. They couldn't help wondering where her humanity lay.

---o---

Back in his room on the ward George resumed his usual occupation of watching cooking programmes, texting Despina, his cousins and friends and posting on Facebook:

"up and walkin already, i swear if physiotherapy was a lesson id be top neek."

He also passed the time receiving his many visitors, taking little walks outside with Dad and Despina or to meet Flash with Mum and Louis, and making small steps towards recovery each day. Just before he was due to be discharged, Mum and Louis brought in a picnic and they all sat out in the sunshine eating and playing with Flash. When the mother superior passed by, they were a little concerned that they would be reprimanded for letting the dog run around, but instead she smiled and pointed them to a large soft ball that someone had abandoned. It was clear where her humanity lay.

During this period, Mum and Louis spent a few sunny afternoons after school walking the dog in the extensive Nonsuch Park, with its fields of long grass and shaded woodland areas. Sometimes they would take a blanket and settle down for sandwiches while throwing a ball for Flash, before returning to the car and continuing on to St Anthony's to visit George and Dad. The world was a beautiful but cruel place.

Finally, George was home again and for the third time they found themselves waiting for the pathology results. Meanwhile, their new oncologist finally agreed to put George on a compromise metronomic therapy. Initially this would involve a low dose oral chemotherapy, plus the anti-inflammatory painkiller, celecoxib. George also had a bone scan and an MRI scan, and an appointment was made to see Mr Hyde. It was a memorable occasion, the day they went to get the pathology results from Mr Hyde. Surely this time everything had been got. Surely?

The wait in the crowded clinic seemed like an age; Dad was on tenterhooks. George was his usual cool self, telling Dad to just calm down; while Mum tried to distract herself with her book. Mr Hyde greeted them brightly and showed them into the consulting room where the usual array of medical personnel was present.

Mr Hyde came straight to the point. The margins were clear; there were no more tumour cells to be seen in the jaw. The relief came over them in a huge wave – and then passed. They didn't know quite how to behave. It was a strange feeling to be hearing such good news finally. It seemed odd to say that it was something of an anti-climax, but it was. Mr Hyde continued to examine George's jaw and other wounds and then they took their leave, still in a daze. They spent the next hour in a trance, having a cup of coffee, then making their way back to the car to set off for home. Mr Hyde had suggested radiotherapy as a follow-up again, but agreed that George could see the radiotherapist at St George's this time. On the way home they were in a strange state of high, but not high. Presumably they just needed time to adjust to the good news.

Such time was not forthcoming. Halfway home, Dad's mobile rang. It was a call from their oncologist at the Royal Marsden and he pulled over to answer it. She informed him that the scans showed an increase in size in the problem spot on the pelvis – at the sacroiliac joint – suggesting that it was almost certainly a metastatic tumour. In addition, there were new spots showing on the right leg. Dad toned down the news for George, underplaying the significance of it all, but it was a huge blow nevertheless. It seemed they weren't to be allowed to celebrate for even one day.

Later that afternoon, Mum and Dad walked the dog in Nonsuch Park and discussed the situation. It was a beautiful sunny day and Flash was enjoying running around to his heart's content. They sat on a bench for a while, going over the details and considering what they could do next. Dad had been looking at treatments in other countries and they began to sift through the possible options with a view to following them up.

Meanwhile, the drug thalidomide was added into George's metronomic treatment, completing the protocol their oncologist had chosen – which had been used by a team at the Marsden in a study carried out a few years previously. Thalidomide was the same drug that had been given to pregnant women in the 1960s for morning sickness and had caused severe damage to their unborn children. However, it was the drug's anti-angiogenic property that made it potentially useful as a tumour inhibitor – paradoxically the same property that had made it so dangerous to developing foetuses. Unfortunately, as it would turn out, it resulted in horrible side-effects for George, and would make his summer very miserable. To his dismay, Dad later discovered, by contacting the originators of this particular protocol in the United States, that it had been abandoned as ineffective. They wondered why their oncologist hadn't known this, or hadn't contacted the original team herself. What was the point in putting George on medication that was already known to be ineffective? Why could she not have adopted the German protocol that seemed to at least be having some success?

By now, Mum and Dad were beginning to get the impression that there was a certain amount of entrenchment amongst UK oncologists. There seemed to be an automatic distrust of any treatments being carried out in another country and a cautiousness in adopting anything that wasn't a standard protocol. One oncologist even said that whatever they might find abroad wouldn't be better than anything they would find in the UK, which was patently not true. Figures for survival of osteosarcoma alone showed that the UK was lagging behind many other developed countries. There were treatments not available in the UK that were given in other countries as standard procedure, such as cryotherapy in the USA. There were innovative procedures being carried out in other places too. For example in Japan, when operating on a cancer patient, dye would be poured over the site of a tumour excision. The dye would adhere to cancer cells, enabling the surgeon to see if there were any tumour cells left behind. And Dad had been looking at a hospital in China. The Fuda Hospital in Guangzhou (formerly Canton) carried out cryoablation, a procedure that attempted to kill tumours through the insertion of needles that were used to apply liquid nitrogen. The doctors there had had some success with this treatment, which was often followed up with immunotherapy. Mum and Dad decided they should make contact with them to discuss George's case.

---o---

It was during this time that George's face began to swell. He already had swelling on the right hand side from the operation, but now he was developing swelling on both sides through water retention. It seemed George was suffering from a known side effect of thalidomide and, consequently, he became unconfident about being seen in public. If he had to go out, he would wear his hood up and cover his face as much as possible. Mum and Dad were concerned for his safety, fearing that his vulnerability would make him a target for bullying.

During this period – since the second and third operations – George had hardly been attending school. It was clear that the isolation was making him very unhappy, and embarrassment about the way he looked was not helping. In addition, the pressure of studying was becoming all too much. He made the decision to retake

Year 12 and to change his subjects. Mum and Dad persuaded him to sit his Psychology AS exam in the meantime and Despina helped him with revision. He took the bus to Sutton a couple of times and they sat in Starbucks and went through his work. Despina was proud to be helping her brother. At this time, he still had gauze on his face from the skin graft, and one day a boy in the coffee shop was repeatedly asking his mum about it in a loud and rude fashion. Despina threatened to go over and say something, but George prevented her. It wasn't his way, to make a fuss. He made a point of ignoring people who stared at him and kept his mind focused on whatever he was doing. Despina was also concerned when she discovered that all the while his leg had been hurting badly, but he was strong-minded and refused to let her ring Dad to come and pick him up, preferring to stick to the plan and take the bus home.

He sat the psychology exam reluctantly and scraped a 'D'. He was in a bad way and began to voice the desire to abandon studying altogether. The family renewed their efforts to persuade him to return to his old school, feeling that this would make a difference. Accordingly, Mum contacted the school and found it was more than willing to have him back. Finally, when he seemed assured that the failure was not his, George took the decision to return. After this he seemed much relieved and visited the art department, with a view to taking an art and design AS. After that, his enthusiasm returned a little and he appeared much happier, especially as he was being warmly greeted as an old mate by pupils from the year previously below him and by staff who seemed genuinely pleased to see him. Louis too was happy that he would be seeing his brother at school. Some of George's confidence seemed to return and he talked up his psychology grade on Facebook and informed his friends of his plan to return to Southborough.

In the meantime, George had other plans. He was nearing his seventeenth birthday and had long wanted to learn to drive. Deprived of living out many aspects of teenagedom, he envisaged himself zipping about in a new Mini Cooper or Volkswagen Scirocco and began making plans to drive to school in the sixth form. As usual, assuming he would succeed in his endeavours, he enquired on Facebook:

"which car should i get, a Mini Cooper or a Suzuki Swift Sport?"

To this end, he started looking for driving lessons. He learnt that he would be eligible for the Motability scheme, which meant he could purchase a new car if he passed his test.

"When I pass my test," said George.

Mum was as doubtful as he was confident. How could he seriously learn to drive when he couldn't walk properly? When his hip gave him pain if he walked too far or did too much exercise? When he couldn't apply pressure properly with his right foot? She thought it was a fantasy. Mum was wrong. Not for the first time George proved the old adage, 'where there's a will there's a way'. He enrolled at a local driving school, sent off for his provisional licence and took his first lesson soon after his seventeenth birthday. He continued with his lessons

throughout the summer, despite his increasingly poor
state, and seemed to be doing very well. Like the prospect
of getting a dog, the thought of driving his own car kept
him going. He began looking at different vehicles,
weighing up the pros and cons, making his choice. Dad
and Despina encouraged him more than Mum; she was
afraid people were pandering to his arrogance, his
unswerving self-belief. Or was it just a quiet
determination not to be beaten down? Was she forgetting
that it was his self-assurance, his determination that had
seen him through so far, in a way that could only be
admired? Besides, he was entitled to have something to
look forward to – a goal to keep him going through all the
hard times.

While George dreamed of cars, Louis was
looking forward to his last day at primary school, but
before that there was the leavers' play to rehearse. They
were putting on a production of 'Cinderella Rockafella'
and Louis had landed the part he coveted – one of the
ugly sisters. Mum, Dad, George and Despina went to
watch the performance one unbearably hot, sticky
evening in July, in the school hall. The long, heavy
drapes were drawn the whole length of the glass doors
and windows looking onto the playground, and it was
stifling. The audience, packed in tight on the rows of
plastic chairs, were fanning themselves with their
programmes or wiping the sweat from their brows. It was
a good production though, and Louis and his performing
co-sister were very funny. Louis was so convincing in his
red dress, high heels and blonde wig that one of the
parents in the audience didn't realise it was actually a boy

underneath the make up!

Shortly after the play and the end of term, it was George's birthday and Mum began making preparations for a surprise party. She and Louis made a birthday cake and hid it, and they secreted other items of food in containers around the house. They piled the fridge high with goodies, while Mum made silly excuses to George, such as:

"Yiayia and Buppou want to come over and give you your presents on Sunday, so we've suggested they stay to eat. I don't want to cook again on Monday, so we're making extra."

George swallowed it whole and it was a great pleasure to see his face when most of the family – Despina, Yiayia, Buppou, aunts, uncles and cousins big and small – piled through the front door on Sunday afternoon. It was a great day on the surface, filled with gifts and adoration for George, but for the adults it was tempered by their knowledge of the deterioration in his health. Dad's family rallied round and tried to be as supportive as they could, but everyone was struggling to cope with the seriousness of the situation.

A photo around that time showed George, in a light grey hoody, now thin and pale, although with a swollen jaw and face, bald head, holding up his mobile phone to take a picture of himself, with a grim expression in his eyes. His former vibrancy seemed absent, as if finally replaced by the heavy burden he was carrying.

---o---

Meanwhile, Mum had been looking for a suitable

place to take a holiday with the boys. George, with his swollen face, didn't want to be seen by strangers and so any usual sort of holiday was out of the question. He was also unable to walk far, even with his crutches, as his hip was now causing him more pain. Mum found a nice, quiet, dog-friendly house out in the countryside, five minutes walk from the River Severn and near the Welsh border. Table tennis and other ball games were provided in the garden and they could spend a week walking the dog, playing tournaments and having barbecues; there was no need to go anywhere much. Trips to the supermarket etc. could be made by Mum or Dad and Louis. Mum booked the cottage for a week in August.

When the time came, the journey to get to the cottage was pretty horrendous. Mum and Dad had come from Suffolk, having spent the weekend with Nanny Olive. An accident on the road delayed them considerably in picking up the boys from Yiayia and Buppou's in South East London. Consequently they didn't leave there until 3.00 p.m. Then, an hour into the next leg of the journey, the traffic on the M25 slowed, eventually coming to a halt. Mum was driving and there was a snap decision, voiced loudly and excitedly by all the passengers, to reverse the car 30 metres back down the motorway and leave by the slip road before the jam became a complete standstill. Apparently there had been an accident that was to cause major problems for the cars that stayed on the motorway. They had lost time, but breathed a sigh of relief that they'd escaped this one. A lorry driver in front of them on the slip road, clearly equally pleased to have got away, was gesticulating and laughing loudly at the queues of cars below who had made the bad choice of staying on the main route.

Unfortunately, it was out of the frying pan, into the fire. The new road produced another accident and further delays. It was nine o'clock in the evening before they finally wound their way down a narrow country lane and pulled into the driveway of the cottage. They were all exhausted and barely able to eat, but relieved to have arrived and very pleased with the house.

Dog walking in the area was easy and they would take it in turns to stroll along nearby paths through fields bordering the river, or wander the country lanes, while someone always stayed with George. Mum picked endless amounts of blackberries and plums, made jar after jar of jam as usual and gathered cooking apples from the tree in the garden. They all did plenty of reading and playing with the dog, who had become very attached to his latest toy – a string of plastic sausages. Each of them would spend time throwing the sausages up the sloping garden and Flash would chase and retrieve them, sometimes catching them in mid-air and getting them tangled up around his snout, much to the amusement of the humans.

But the week provided a mixture of pleasure and concern. George was becoming increasingly depressed, as the swelling on his face showed no signs of receding. In addition, the most recent skin graft on his leg was taking longer than expected to heal. He joined in table tennis and other games, with his usual focus and aplomb and tucked into barbecues, but somehow his heart was not in it. It was upsetting and worrying to watch. Mum and Dad could find no way of helping him. He slept late and became surly and uncommunicative at times.

On the day they left, they took a detour, to see something of the Forest of Dean and then Wales, returning over the breezy Severn Bridge, before taking the motorway home. In the Forest of Dean they stopped for a walk with the dog. George came too, supporting himself on his two crutches, swinging himself wildly through the deserted woods. He insisted on climbing a tree-covered hill and plunging down into the bracken on the other side, flying over the undergrowth like some kind of maniac let loose after a long period of incarceration. Mum and Dad were terrified he'd fracture his increasingly fragile hip, but he was not to be halted. It was as if he had regained all his heroic strength and ability to transcend his situation for just this one walk. They got lost and fought their way back through the greenery and over fallen logs, until they spotted the car. Ironically, it was Mum who fell over and grazed her shin badly. On the motorway home they stopped for a not very nice meal and George sat in the service station café, with his hood pulled over his face, eating quickly and quietly. It was heartbreaking to see someone so young, once so vibrant and outgoing, hiding away as if he was trying to make himself invisible to the world. What a far cry from the fleetingly wild, free boy in the woods earlier.

Back home his leg swelled up to match his face. Before they went to Southwold for their summer stay the oncologist stopped the thalidomide to see if the problem would clear up. Mum and Dad cursed the drug that hadn't been part of the German protocol which they had wanted.

---o---

They left for their Southwold trip on Saturday 21st August 2010. This time they were in a property they hadn't stayed in before. It was a big house, set back from the road, at the furthest end of the high street from the sea. It had been a bit of an expensive mistake by Mum, who had misunderstood the price at the time of booking. It was modernised, with a large, open-plan kitchen, dining and sitting room on the ground floor, plus a wide, walled, terraced garden, sporting plenty of chairs, loungers and a large wooden table. The floors were also wooden, which was not so comfortable in the bedrooms upstairs. The top half of the bedroom doors were of translucent glass, making them see-through when the light was on, plus the floors made it noisy and there was an awkward step down to the bathroom, which was difficult for George to negotiate. However, it was well-equipped, the boys liked its modern open-plan style and it was conveniently situated just five minutes walk from the sea.

By Monday George's leg wound, where the second skin graft had been taken, was in a weepy, messy state. The skin that had been re-growing had started to break down and the wound was beginning to open up. Dad took him to James Paget Hospital, a fifty-minute drive away. Fortunately they had a letter from the Marsden, allowing them to jump the queues in A&E, but it was lunchtime before they were back. The wound had been examined and the dressing changed. There had been so many different dressings tried on this second leg wound, but nothing really seemed to help. They cursed the thalidomide again. Why would any doctor give an anti-angiogenic drug to a patient who had a major wound to heal? They only hoped that now the drug had been stopped the swellings would recede and the wound would begin to heal again.

For the rest of the week George stayed at home. He had no desire to be seen in public and only once came down to the beach hut they rented, to say a brief hello to their friends. Dad stayed with him for long periods of time and they all spent more time at the house than they would normally have done. George was also suffering from periods of itching again and consequent insomnia. His face was swollen, his leg was swollen, his skin-graft wound was in a bad way and he was not in a holiday mood. Eating out was off the agenda and in addition he suffered with a bad stomach for a couple of days. He had lost a lot of weight over the two years of illness, but had grown in height and his clothes hung loosely on him. He didn't look at all well. He wasn't at all well.

---o---

When they returned home from Southwold, they discovered that their oncologist was on leave for personal reasons and was to be replaced by a young woman in her thirties, who had also been part of the team at UCH headed by the leading osteosarcoma doctor they hadn't hit it off with. They tried to put their prejudices aside.

At this point, Louis went away on a short residential trip with the new Year Seven pupils – prior to starting school proper. It was a time of getting to know other boys and some of the teachers in a context of various outdoor activities. It was a tradition at the school that George had also experienced and Louis loved it. He came home on the Friday afternoon, tired and muddy, but happy.

On Monday he started school and on Tuesday George started sixth form. Louis was pleased to be able to pass his brother in the corridor and nod a brief greeting to him, and to come home and discuss the idiosyncrasies of the various teachers who had also taught George. They would swap notes and George let Louis into the secret of a few nicknames.

But the problems were ongoing for George. Although the facial swelling was reducing, he was now becoming jaundiced – just as he was starting back at school. Regular blood tests showed that his bilirubin count was ascending fast, suggesting a problem in the liver. Fortunately, an ultrasound indicated there were no tumours present, but all drugs were stopped to give his liver a chance to recover. Dad was afraid it was a sign of general acceleration in tumour growth.

Meanwhile, Dad had been reading about a substance that was being manufactured, called GcMAF, which exists in the body as a normal part of the immune system. It is suggested that GcMAF activates immune cells to destroy cancer cells, but that tumours subvert the immune system to prevent this from happening. A small amount of research had already been carried out, in rats and in a few humans, which involved giving manufactured GcMAF to enable the immune system to be activated to start killing cancer cells. Dad obtained some of the substance, but after a few weeks with no results, George stopped taking it. Later, Dad realised that there was a good deal of controversy as to whether certain producers were able to supply an effective version of this substance. Later still some of the original papers describing GcMAF were retracted (withdrawn) by the journals that had first published them.

During this period George also had several scans taken of the pelvis and leg, a biopsy of the pelvis at Stanmore Hospital and an ultrasound of his abdomen. Whilst the experts at Stanmore considered the spots on the leg to be due to post-surgical trauma, they confirmed that there was high-grade osteosarcoma present on the pelvis.

---o---

The new oncologist told George he couldn't be cured. It was a bombshell from which Mum and Dad had tried to protect him. He took it in his stride during the appointment, but on the way home he began asking some questions, although he was still not very vocal. Mum and Dad said they hadn't reached the end of the line yet, but it was a difficult conversation. Then he sat in the back of the car, large green headphones on, listening to his music. In the last few months of his life, he was to abandon listening to music completely because of the emotional effect. Perhaps it was too much of a reminder of the life he had once had and how far he had become removed from it.

When they arrived home, George went straight upstairs and Dad followed. George was crying – crying out. Mum sat limply at the foot of the stairs, not wishing to invade their intimacy, not sure if George would want her there – and listened. It was the sound of someone terrified for his life. She had only heard that sound once before, when a blackbird was caught by a peregrine falcon in the back garden. It had screamed for its life in the same shocking way, with a tone like nothing she had ever heard before. With the bird, she had been unable to stand it and had interfered in nature, had run out waving a chair madly to frighten away the bird of prey. Now George, their son, was crying out in the same desperate way and this time she just sat uselessly, helplessly on the stairs, listening.

Finally the cries subsided leaving only the sound of quiet sobbing coming from George and Dad. Gradually that too petered out and there was silence. Mum knew it was the silence of Dad comforting George, his arms wrapped around his son as his heart broke. Eventually Mum went up and knocked gently on the door. She went in, held George for a minute and sat quietly with them for a while, as normal conversation returned and they once again reassured George that they hadn't reached the end of the line.

Meanwhile George wasn't receiving any treatment, as there were still concerns about his liver. Dad renewed contact with China and they discussed with George the possibility of making the trip. Whilst George had been nervous and reluctant at first, he was now adamant that he should travel to Fuda Hospital in Guangzhou. Dad sent off copies of scans and queued at the Chinese embassy in London to obtain visas for him and George. They made their plans and it was agreed that George and Dad would go, while Mum and Louis would stay at home, so that Louis could continue to attend school and Flash could be looked after. Also, the treatment, which would take place over a period of four weeks, was expensive and they needed to keep the costs of travel and accommodation to a minimum. They would once again use the money invested for the children when George's mother had died, but Yiayia and Buppou would pay the airfare.

It was a brave and daunting thing for George to do – heroic even. His friends on Facebook were amazed. And rightly so. He would travel halfway round the world to a country where he didn't speak the language or have any understanding of the culture, to put his trust in doctors he had never met and with whom he couldn't communicate. The journey alone would be exhausting in his weak state. He was going into the unknown. But what choice did he really have? To give up and prepare to die at the age of seventeen? That was not George's way. If China offered the only possible chance of defeating this disease, then he would go to China, and once his mind was made up, he was impatient to get on with it. It would be an adventure, with his dad by his side; they were a team and would rise to the occasion together.

And Dad? He was terrified. What if this wasn't the right decision? What if George couldn't cope? What if the treatment didn't work? The tension built as the countdown to departure began. Mum and Louis were dreading the parting; Despina was dreading it; Yiayia and Buppou and the rest of the family too. Everyone was filled with apprehension and a desperate need to believe that this treatment would work. If not, what else was there? The new consultant oncologist had made her position clear – George was not curable and could only be offered palliative care from now on; it was time to come to terms with his mortality and strive to keep him symptom free and able to participate in school and family life for as long as possible. She did not consider the trip advisable; she appeared to think it was a waste of time and would take its toll on George. But she wished him well all the same. Once again, the family felt very alone. They focused on making preparations for the trip and the countdown began.

13. Snake and Black Chicken

The days leading up to the China trip were tense. It seemed such a very long wait, but finally bags were packed, passports, visas and tickets were in order, medication had been sorted and the day of departure arrived. It had been decided that Mum would drive Dad and George to the airport, accompanied by Louis and Despina. Mum, who dreaded a long drawn out leave-taking, would have preferred to see them off from home in a taxi, but Dad wanted her to drive them and Despina and Louis wanted to go. Most importantly, George wanted them all to be there when he left.

And so it was that on the morning of Saturday 2nd October 2010 George said his goodbyes to Flash, and the humans set off once again in the family Zafira, this time for Heathrow Airport. It was still fairly warm for an October day (by the time they returned from China it would be cold and rainy) and Dad and George were anticipating hot weather in China. The flight was at 1.00 p.m. and they were in good time and hoped to be able to avoid a long wait at check-in, as George couldn't stand up for very long.

At the airport, they parked in the short-stay, multi-storey car park and made their way down in the lift to the busy departures hall. Luckily, George was waved through check-in fairly swiftly and they all went for a coffee while they waited for the flight to be called. The airport was bustling as usual, with passengers setting off for long-awaited holidays, businessmen clutching briefcases, excited children running around and departure announcements regularly punctuating the general background noise. Mum found the wait tortuous; each second was an age, as they sat drinking their coffee and exchanging small talk. But at last the announcement came for the twelve-hour flight that Dad and George were to take to Hong Kong, before changing and picking up the short flight to Guangzhou. It was time to say goodbye.

Mum, Louis and Despina kissed and hugged George and Dad in turn. Despina was in tears; Louis was in tears too. Mum held on to hers, knowing that if she started she wouldn't be able to make the drive home. She turned away quickly as father and son passed through the barrier and gradually disappeared amongst the other travellers. She kept a tight grip, concentrating her mind on practical details – the way out of the airport, the leak in the kitchen ceiling to be dealt with on her return, Flash to be walked. She made her way, with Despina and Louis, back up the lift to the car and they navigated their way out of the airport on to the busy A4 to begin their journey home. There was a lot of traffic and from then on they focused mainly on getting into the correct lanes and taking the right turnings, but there was a feeling of emptiness that was already beginning to seep into each person's consciousness.

Once they were safely home, Mum gave in at last, sinking into a numb, heavy, listlessness. While Louis and Despina went upstairs to watch a DVD, she sat on the sofa in the sitting room, not moving a muscle, staring into space. She sat there for a full half-hour; her brain was numb, she wasn't even aware of thinking. They had gone – for a number of weeks. She began to reflect. How would George cope? How would Panik (using Dad's real name here, as she always did) cope, dealing with it all without her? They had always been together, supporting each other through everything. How would she cope knowing she couldn't be there to support Panik and George? How in heaven's name had they come to this?

After half an hour she stood up, went to her desk, sat down and opened her laptop. She created a new file and began typing. She typed her feelings, her fears, and she spoke to Panik in her writing. Gradually the words became chattier and when she came to a halt three pages later she felt better; some sort of transition had occurred, enabling her to move on. Each evening after that she would write to Panik – a little diary for the day. Because of the time difference (China being seven hours ahead) it would arrive when he was in bed asleep, but it would be there for him when he got up the next day. It was a help – this diary, this communication – to keep them both going. Mum would go off to sleep, imagining Panik just waking up to read her account of the day. And the following morning she would rise and go straight to her laptop to read his reply, sent in the middle of her night.

On that first day, Louis went into Kingston with his sister. They ate in Frankie and Benny's: pasta and sauce each and shared dessert, all for a tenner. It was their 'thing' to do that. In years to come, they would go to Wetherspoon's for Sunday breakfast. It was good, cheap and filling according to Louis – but not as nice as Mum's.

Louis returned feeling a little guilty that he had left Mum alone, but she said it was ok. Actually, she was relieved in some ways to have had the house to herself to collect her thoughts. That evening though, after Despina had gone, mother and son settled down together to watch a film. They were cosy, close – alone but together in their new adventure – and they would be ok. Louis asked if Mum was ok and she said she was fine.

That night Louis sobbed and Mum held him; he felt it now. She suggested he make a mark on his calendar every morning so that he could see the days passing. And she guaranteed it would pass and soon they would all be back together again. That's what she always said when one of the kids was hurt or upset "it will pass" – to try and help them to see beyond the present difficulty. Louis wondered if the treatment was going to help George, and Mum said they must hope so. They held each other close and he fell asleep from exhaustion. Then Mum went to bed alone and cried too.

---o---

Dad and George spent much of the long flight to

Hong Kong watching movies. As usual George homed in on the comedies and at one point he was laughing so much that Dad was drawn into watching Kick Ass with him. In between, they dozed, ate in-flight food and chatted briefly about nothing in particular. As the plane descended into Hong Kong airport they gazed at the spectacular view – a multitude of skyscrapers set right up against the sea. So far, so good.

The problems started in Hong Kong: the flight to Guangzhou was cancelled. The airline presented them with the choice of either waiting around for another flight or taking the bus to Guangzhou. They opted for the latter and were surprised to be invited to board an impressively fancy, shiny, comfortable, brand new people carrier, boasting excellent air conditioning. It took them through the border with China to Shenzhen, another bustling, commercial city with impressive sky lines. They began to relax and enjoy travelling in style.

In Shenzhen they realised their naïve mistake. The people carrier was taking them to the coach station, where they were summarily dismissed along with their luggage, with strict instructions to board a certain coach from a particular pick-up point at a specific time. They were abandoned amongst the crowds, with few other foreigners in sight and no reassuring signs in English, while buses pulled in and out of the busy station in every direction. Standing amongst the groups of waiting travellers, the air conditioning they had enjoyed in the fancy car a thing of the past, they began to feel the effects of the heat and humidity.

Eventually a coach arrived at the allotted time and they joined in the scramble to store their cases and get aboard, Dad attempting to ensure that George was not too battered in the crush. There was none of the polite queuing that at least people paid lip-service to in England. Were they even on the right coach? The driver glanced at their tickets and waved them to their seats. What a contrast to the luxurious people-carrier! They spent the next couple of hours wending their way through the Chinese countryside, sweating in the tropical heat, wriggling and adjusting themselves in the none-too-comfy seats, while being thrown around by suspension that had definitely seen better days. Although they were the only Westerners on board, no one paid them much attention and they passed the time taking in the sights of the lush, green countryside, studded with paddy fields and small plots of vegetables; they hadn't realised just how tropical it would be. The motorway skirted several small towns, none of them on the scale of Hong Kong or Shenzhen and not nearly as modern and impressive.

Once they reached Guangzhou, Dad's concern became how to get to Fuda hospital. The city seemed to sprawl for miles, with crowded streets, busy markets and shops, and they had no idea where they were going to be dropped off. George was his usual self, unstressed by all this and keen to drink everything in. He was busy trying to work out whether they drove on the left or right in China, as it was decidedly unclear and there were also an equal number of left-hand and right-hand drive vehicles to be seen. At the same time, the roads seemed to be catering for heavily laden, ageing bicycles, labouring alongside spanking-new speeding Mercedes and BMWs.

Eventually, they were let down at a busy intersection in the middle of the city, and they proceeded to drag their heavy cases along while trying to decide what to do next. Suddenly, Dad spotted a luxury hotel. Perhaps they might speak English there? To get to it, they had to negotiate the busy main road and avoid being mown down by the relentless stream of traffic. Having crossed and remained in one piece, they entered the hotel lobby, which was full of people milling around or talking loudly on their mobile phones. George was fascinated by a Manga-style mural on the wall, created in honour of the Asian Games, which were shortly to be hosted in Guangzhou. He was extremely fond of Manga art as well as graphic novels and had a sizeable collection of both at home.

Dad left him taking photos and went to convince the man behind the desk to call Fuda Hospital, which he eventually agreed to do. This did not produce the immediate success that Dad had hoped for as, apparently, it was a public holiday and there seemed to be nobody about. Fortunately, after a while, the hotel receptionist succeeded in getting through to someone who knew about Dad and George. A car had already been sent to collect them from Guangzhou Airport, but it was soon diverted and finally they were installed in the back seats and on their way to the hospital. George attempted to photograph the impressive TV tower as they passed it, as well as other local sights that took his fancy. Dad was just relieved to be finally heading for the hospital where treatment was to happen.

When they arrived at Fuda, they found themselves gazing at a broad, twelve-storey, concrete building on the intersection of a long, wide road, south west of the centre of Guangzhou. The architecture was Stalinist – functional, unexciting and looking more like the headquarters of a provincial bank than a hospital. They made their way to the entrance, which was decked with flags and banners, passing the security guards by the door as they went in. Inside they found a large waiting area at reception and a row of cashier stations similar to a bureau de change or a bank, where patients could pay for their treatment. As they would discover later, most of the Chinese patients who queued here were outpatients, while there were Filipino and other Asian patients, plus some Westerners, accommodated in rooms on some of the upper floors.

Dad and George were taken up to the third floor, where they were shown into a self-contained suite consisting of a bedroom, a sitting room and a bathroom with a walk-in shower. First impressions were that it was functional in style and lower tech than hospitals back home. As they entered the large beige and white bedroom, there was a hospital bed for George on one side and a bed for Dad on the other, plus a small table and chairs. The small sitting-room was furnished with a hard-looking black sofa, a coffee table, a TV and some storage space. The bathroom had a kind of utility area for hanging up washing and preparing food and a hot water machine was provided for making hot drinks. They were able to eat, sleep and hang up their washing, but it was somewhat lacking home comforts. In the days to come, they would give up using the sitting room, as the sofa turned out to be decidedly uncomfortable, especially for George. From then on they would spend most of their time propped up on their beds, with George on the Internet or texting his sister, while Dad attempted to do some work on his laptop. But for now, the two travellers flopped down on the somewhat firm beds and decided to catch up on some sleep. It was mid-afternoon on Sunday and they had been travelling for almost 24 hours.

---o---

Back home, it was only Sunday morning and Louis had a football match to go to. Mum downloaded a map from the Internet and planned the route to the away team's ground. On the way, Louis did a good job of navigating because, unlike Dad, he knew his left from his right. When they arrived, she sat in the car for a bit, while the teams warmed up. Then she had a glorious time, standing in the pouring rain watching Louis's team lose 9-1. Still, the flask of hot milky coffee at half-time helped – and at least there was a loo at this ground.

When they got home, later than expected, she had to deal with the leak in the roof of the kitchen extension. It was still raining lightly, but she needed to go outside and identify what was causing the problem. Louis held the extension ladder while Mum ascended to the flat roof, climbed on to it and pulled the ladder up. She converted it to a stepladder and climbed again, to have a look at the chimney on the main roof, where the damage seemed to be. However, in the middle of her inspection they heard the sound of Dad calling on Skype. Louis dashed indoors, so as not to miss the call, while Mum struggled to collapse the stepladder and convert it to extension again, in order to lower it back down to ground level.

Damn! It was several inches short of the ground; she hadn't extended it enough. Dilemma – should she risk letting it drop the last six inches, hoping that she didn't lose it, and then stretch the necessary amount to climb down on to it, or should she hoist it back up? In the end she chose the latter course, fearing that the ladder might fall and Louis might not be able to pick it up again. She had to adopt a new level of responsibility, which meant abandoning her usual reckless behaviour in such situations. She struggled to extend the ladder the necessary amount, and finally climbed down, wet from the rain and covered in black gunk from the roof. At least she was in time to catch a few words with Panik.

Panik said there would be no translator until Monday and so communication with hospital personnel was extremely difficult. Mum worried about him and George coping, but Panik said they were doing ok. It was good to talk. He put the call on speaker and she had a few words with George too. Thank goodness Panik had set up Skype for them. After their conversation, Mum made herself French onion soup, which no one else liked, and sat down to read with a glass of wine. Reading made her feel closer to Panik, who was an extensive consumer of the printed word.

---o---

In China over the next few days Dad and George explored a little. They discovered that their floor was home to a ward, which contained a nurses' station where the nurses sat in their light-pink uniforms, doctors' offices where the doctors sat in their white coats and next to that an open plan waiting room. Following the faded carpet down one of the corridors they found treatment rooms, while the private rooms where they were accommodated were situated along another corridor. Most of the patients seemed to keep to themselves, but Dad and George began to chat to one other patient – a woman in her mid-30s from the UK, but who was ethnically Chinese, as were most of the foreign patients – that or from the Philippines. She had metastatic endometrial cancer that was inoperable and, like many of the foreigners, she had come to Fuda because she had no other treatment on offer. She had arrived that same weekend and had left her two children back home in the UK. Over the ensuing weeks, discussions between her and Dad would reveal a picture of Fuda that did not necessarily live up to the expectations it had raised.

On the Monday, George was taken for scans – an ultra sound, a CT scan of his pelvis and a chest X-ray. He was also started on an infusion to help his liver, which would continue all week and limit his mobility somewhat, but he was still able to wander the corridors while hooked up to the drip, or venture out when he was unhooked.

Opposite the hospital, and to one side of it, there were blocks of flats crowded together, with windows fluttering with washing. The flats were not at all run down and certainly not as depressing as some of the estates in London. Occasionally, Dad and George would see groups of elderly people in the courtyard doing Tai Chi in the morning. One day they were taken into the estate by one of the translators, a Filipino woman who had worked in Manchester before moving to China with her husband. They browsed in the market square, which boasted a selection of small shops and stalls selling produce to the locals. There were all kinds of exotic foods on display, but George was disappointed that there were none of the cheap electronic goods he hankered after.

They settled into a routine, which was to last about ten days until treatment began. Each morning they would be woken at around 7.30 with breakfast, which consisted of either dumplings or rice with a little prawn or chicken. They would wash or shower and then wander over to the corner shop on the housing estate. Here they would pick up tea bags for Dad, snacks or essentials like toilet paper – not supplied by the hospital. The shop was about the size of a local Londis in the UK and the shelves were stacked high with goods, including plenty of fresh produce, and there were fridges full of meat and cold drinks. George was as fascinated as ever by yet another intriguing new place, where the items on sale were so cheap. He began making lists of things he wanted to purchase to take back home – vacuum-packed chicken claws for his sister, badly-made fake designer underwear for his friends and a small dagger in a scabbard for himself. Unfortunately, apart from the dagger, which he bought in the first week, he was unable to make the other purchases, as he became too immobile to return to the shop after treatment began. From then on, it was down to Dad to quickly run across and stock up on tea bags, soap or whatever else they needed.

During that first week, however, they also made a trip into the centre of Guangzhou. George was desperate to find some kind of fancy gadget for himself. He knew that the iPad and other tablet computers were manufactured in China and he was aware that cheap copies of these were also to be found. It was the latter he was looking for, and so they asked the nurses where they might go to purchase such a thing. The nurses clearly misunderstood what they were after because they were directed to a smart, westernised store in a shopping centre on one of the main roads in the city centre. The shopping mall was full of small shops specialising in high-tech equipment – the official outlets for iPads and iPods, laptops by Lenovo and Sony, cameras by Nikon. George soon became exhausted from traipsing around and his back was aching badly. In the end, completely fatigued, irritated and unwilling to admit defeat, he bought a new camera to take pictures for his art project at school, but in reality he could have picked it up in Tesco for a similar price. Following this, they looked for somewhere to eat, but were to be equally disappointed by the worst and easily most expensive meal they would eat in their whole stay in China. Having decided to opt for something completely Western for a change, they seated themselves next to groups of prosperous-looking Chinese people in Pizza Hut, where they ordered piles of food to restore their energy, only to find that the ingredients had been altered to appeal to the Chinese palate. The exorbitantly-priced food just did not taste right; the tomato sauce was oddly spiced and the whole pizza tasted very strange. They returned to Fuda, weary, unsatisfied and with George in considerable pain.

During those early days at the hospital they also liked to take the lift to the upper floors and then climb the last two flights of stairs up to the roof where, in one of the small buildings the 'Western Restaurant' was located. It was really more of a small café with a few tables and chairs, serving a decidedly Chinese version of Western food. In the other buildings they discovered a communal kitchen – where Chinese and Filipino patients would prepare food – and a gym, which was really just a room full of rusting equipment that had seen better days.

Outside on the roof though was an impressive roof garden, decked out with palms and other exotic greenery and with several small ponds, which boasted little colonies of terrapins that George was most interested in – so much so that he began enquiring as to whether he could purchase some for his bedroom when they returned home. Together, Dad and George would lean on the chest-high wall that bordered the garden at the edge of the roof and gaze out at the stunning view. From here they could see right across Guangzhou, with its higgledy-piggledy mix of skyscrapers dotted amongst the low housing estates. Everywhere there was new construction taking place and the whole of Guangzhou seemed to consist of a random mix of the old and new. It was not unusual to see cyclists travelling down six-lane motorways against the oncoming traffic, or to find individuals selling a couple of squashes, or some other little pile of produce, on the side of a busy, main road somewhere.

The hospital was one of the tall modern buildings, but across the road in the older housing estate, amongst the shops there was a café. Later on, when George could no longer climb the stairs up to the roof, meals were cooked to order by this café and served in their room. Or sometimes, if they had missed out on ordering food while George was in treatment, Dad would wander over to the café and point at the dishes he wanted to buy.

The menu from the café consisted of a number of culinary dishes that would make many westerners' hair stand on end, but George tried and enjoyed them all – rat, snake, frog, black chicken. When they enquired as to the source of the snake, they were assured that it was not wild, but 'man-made', presumably meaning that, like the rat, it was farmed. The black chicken was actually black through and through, but the meat tasted just like any other chicken. The food was often spicy and served in a soup or with rice. Dad enjoyed much of the food too, but after a month of this diet, they began to long for a bowl of Mum's bean and pasta soup, or some fish pie, quiche, lamb shepherd's pie with mustard mash, a nice glass of wine... However, the worst aspect of culinary deprivation for Dad was the lack of a good, strong cup of tea – tea with that deep tan colour that only a good Assam can produce. Add a splash of milk and Dad was in tea heaven. Sadly, the lighter-style Chinese teas just didn't appeal to his palate and his cravings went unsatisfied. No matter; all this paled into insignificance next to his worries about George.

---o---

By the end of the first week, George's liver function was returning to normal, but Dad told Mum on Skype that the CT scan showed the tumour on the pelvis as considerably enlarged – in Dad's words, "massive." Dad was relieved that George hadn't seen the images, as he had been hooked up to the drip dispensing the medicine with which his liver was being treated. According to Dad, the scan looked "as scary as hell." This did not bode well. Dad was edgy; he was worried that they would revise and reduce the treatment options. It would not be until after the PET scan at the beginning of the second week, however, that a final treatment plan would be put together.

Despite this, on the Friday of the first week George was given a treatment called Cancer Micro-vascular Intervention (CMI), which involved a procedure similar to that which George underwent in Germany, but fortunately not nearly as frightening. Chemotherapy drugs were mixed with other chemicals to create a 'lumpy drug', which was then pumped into the tumour along with a dye, via a line inserted into an artery. The large molecules meant that the chemo would become trapped in the tumour, where it would act to destroy it. In a procedure that was over very quickly, the drug was pumped into George's pelvis. The only noteworthy aspect of the whole process was that the surgeon didn't speak a word of English and neither did his assistant. As the translators were not around that day, George and Dad had to rely on sign language for communication, which was a little unnerving at times.

---o---

Back home in the UK, at the end of the first week Mum and Louis drove up to see Nanny Olive. Mum took him out of school on the Friday and they made a long weekend of it, getting in some good walks on the beach with Flash. Louis was good company and she was happy to have him there. The trip took them out of themselves and they both seemed to feel better, but when they returned home on Sunday night the house felt even more empty and lonely. Still, one week had passed. However, Panik had told her that their stay was going to be extended, as it had taken over a week to get the PET scan done, which Dad hadn't anticipated from the information he had been given before setting off for China. They would now be away for more than five weeks. Mum would have to find a way to break it to Louis.

---o---

On Tuesday of the second week, George was taken to the Sun Yat Sen University hospital for a PET scan. The results received the following day were not good. They confirmed a large area of tumour on the pelvis and, in addition, a hot spot was located in his throat. Although the doctors examined George and could feel nothing there, this was now adding a new area of concern. On Thursday, when George had his first treatment of cryoablation therapy, the doctor showed Dad a picture on a screen of where the dye had spread through the tiny blood vessels in the pelvic tumour. It revealed a frightening picture of a vast and dense spider's web deep inside George's pelvis.

Unfortunately, the first cryoablation treatment caused problems; severe damage to a nerve manifested itself in numbness and a permanent inability to lift the right leg. Dad was worried: this was not a good start. George's overriding concern was that it would interfere with his driving lessons. At this time, it was also decided he should have a treatment of brachytherapy (a form of radiotherapy that involved injecting beads of radio-active material directly into the tumour). He suffered greatly from the after effects of these two treatments, with huge amounts of inflammation, high temperatures and extreme pain when passing urine.

---o---

Back in London it was Louis's birthday; he was twelve, nearly a teenager! Mum thought, "Here we go again…"

Actually Louis's birthday had happened before Dad and George went away, but he was having his birthday 'party' a little later on, when the film he wanted to see was showing at the cinema. He had arranged to watch the film with a few friends and go for a pizza afterwards. Mum would see them into the cinema and then she would leave them to watch the film, while she did some shopping, before returning to get them installed in the Pizza Express. They set off for Kingston with one friend in tow. They met a second friend at the top of the escalators in the busy Rotunda in Kingston – a leisure complex, comprising a bowling alley in the basement, several restaurants and fourteen screens in the Odeon upstairs. They waited some time for the last two to arrive.

Mum knew that Ronnie, one of Louis's friends was large for his age and that the other friend had similar, curly hair and although not as large as Ronnie, was quite big for his age too. Still, her heart sank when she saw the pair of them coming up the escalators munching on pink candyfloss and looking much older than Louis and every bit like trouble. She was concerned about how they would behave in the cinema once they all got together, but in the end she decided to leave them to it and stop worrying. What would be would be. Kids needed some freedom, without parents fussing around all the time.

Mum did some shopping, bought a jumper and a couple of other small items and returned to rendezvous with the boys. After searching high and low, she sent a text to Louis, who confirmed that they were, of course, not where she had instructed them to meet her. Finally, she got them seated in the busy Pizza Express, gave Louis the money-off vouchers that she had obtained and went off for another bout of shopping. By the time she came back to the restaurant she was bored silly with shopping.

The boys were seated at a round table in the middle of the busy restaurant and were in high spirits. She had been wrong about trouble though. Ronnie especially was extremely polite and as nice as pie. Louis looked happy with his friends and Mum was happy for him too. It was good to see him enjoying himself, given everything he had to cope with at home.

After the restaurant, she drove them all back to the house to wait for their parents to pick them up. She had pulled out a couple of bottles of wine to offer the parents, but mostly people were in a hurry. The boys played football in the driveway at the side of the house and one of them managed to step in some dog poo that Mum didn't realise Flash had left. She spent fifteen minutes cleaning the boy's trainer, while apologising profusely to his granddad who had come to pick him up. When everyone had gone, she sat down with a large glass of wine and wrote her diary for the day to send to Panik. It had been a tiring but successful day and Louis thanked her for it.

Although Mum found it difficult to get a real picture of what it was like for Dad and George in China, she sensed that things were getting harder as the weeks passed. It was strange to be in a different world from the two of them while all this was happening. The days dragged on back home, as they appeared to for Dad and George. One morning when she woke it felt as if they had been away for a month and, although she had stopped counting the days, she was shocked nonetheless to find that it had only been 2 weeks. Louis was finding it hard too, but he cheered Mum up by coming to her and saying:

"We'll get through Mum; we make a good team."

And he was right of course, they would get through; they had to.

Mum's birthday arrived and it was a quiet affair. Despina had asked if she wanted to go out for dinner, but she didn't really feel like it. She missed Panik, but she and Louis did have tea and huge cream cakes in a patisserie in Kingston and that was nice. Natasha popped round with a present and Louis brought out some presents from George and Dad that they had hidden away before they went to China.

Louis and Mum grew closer. It was not just a case of Mum supporting Louis and making sure he was ok; he supported her too. He was a friend and a comfort, he was a helper and he was there beside her, coping with it all. The China period was one of the hardest times and they missed Dad and George terribly. Louis helped in the house, navigated Mum to football matches early on Sunday mornings, held the ladder for the roof inspection, walked the dog with her and hugged her when she needed it.

Over the weeks, they worked their way through episodes of 'Fawlty Towers' on DVD, saving one for each time they sat together to eat in front of the TV. They never watched more than one at a time because they needed to keep a new one to look forward to for as long as possible. It helped. They visited Nanny Olive twice, taking strong milky coffee and biscuits for the journey, so that Mum could have a break from driving. They walked the dog on the beach and took photos with their mobiles, of the waves in wild weather. Of course, there were times when Louis got irritated with her for laying down the rules, but he forgave her in the end. They liked each other and needed each other and couldn't be enemies for long.

---o---

In the third week, George had more cryotherapy, followed by his first immunotherapy injection. He was also being treated with acupuncture for the pain. His nights were disturbed and they were informed that there was evidence of lung metastases on the PET scan. In week four his appetite began to decrease and the pain and discomfort were bringing him near to breaking point. In one email to Mum, Dad described him as crying and shaking with pain.

One positive piece of news punctuated the otherwise worsening scenario. The scan after the follow-up CMI treatment painted a completely different picture. The spread of the dye was a fraction of what it had been, indicating that the pelvic tumour was dying back and showing that many of the fine blood vessels had collapsed. Everyone hoped that perhaps Fuda could still make a big difference to George's chances of survival. Dad wondered if the CMI had been the biggest factor in the killing of tumour cells. Ironically, it was the one treatment the hospital didn't really talk up and it certainly wasn't the one George and Dad had travelled half way round the world for. But apart from this one positive scan result, as the weeks passed the news from China was not good. During his stay there, George underwent repeat treatments of cryoablation, had four immunotherapy injections, brachytherapy, some acupuncture and two treatments of CMI.

As time passed, George's hip was becoming increasingly painful and the only day that he and his dad had ventured into the city centre had resulted in exhaustion and pain for the next twenty-four hours. As the weeks passed he became less and less mobile and spent most of his time, when not in treatment, lying in his bed. Perhaps they just hadn't realised how much the treatments would affect George, or perhaps it was also that the pelvic tumour had grown and was increasingly causing problems and that the disease had further metastasised. The treatments themselves often caused either severe pain or high temperatures, and of course there was the damaged nerve in his leg. By the beginning of the fifth week he was being given morphine, followed later in the week by an injection of prednisolone into his pelvis, in an attempt to ease the now severe pain. Although his mobility improved a little after this, he remained nauseous, which they were later to learn was the result of severe constipation. The doctors enquired frequently as to the efficacy of their patient's bowel movements, but George found the questions intrusive and irritating and often did not answer with complete honesty. The opiate-based painkillers that he was now being prescribed were to eventually result in faecal impaction and cause him considerable pain and sickness by the time he returned home. On the positive side, the CT scan had indicated that a large percentage of the tumour on the pelvis had been killed. Could the remaining cells be annihilated by the injections of immunotherapy?

On the whole, the care George received at Fuda Hospital was good. However, it was expensive, and Dad began to feel that they had not exactly been brought there on false pretences, but that they were being somewhat taken advantage of as Westerners who were able to pay.

He began to agree with the other UK patient they chatted with that the hospital didn't live up to all it proclaimed in its publicity. First of all, the proposed treatment plan had changed once George arrived and was seen by a doctor. Although this was not especially unusual, Dad had been led to understand that George would arrive one day, be taken for a PET scan the next and then treatment would begin. Instead, they were booked in during a holiday period when none of these things could take place and, consequently, they waited more than a week for the PET scan. Perhaps there would still have been delays to sort out George's liver function, but if the scan had been taken earlier treatment would have been moved forward a number of days at least. The cost to the family was increased by these delays. There was a feeling that the doctors were cramming in every possible treatment, at great cost to the patient; the bill was mounting every day. Fortunately, Dad was presented with a tally each day, before he had to make any decisions about proceeding with the next treatment, and so at least there was no chance of a nasty surprise at the end of their stay. Accommodation, food, treatment and care was all included and itemised daily.

However, there seemed to be a certain lack of honesty about treatment – with immunotherapy being the worst example. Cultures of George's osteosarcoma cells were supposed to provide testing material to give an idea whether the vaccine was likely to work, but when Dad asked how the cultures were reacting, he was informed that they were unable to culture bone tumour samples. Why then had they not taken samples of the soft tissue that the tumour had invaded? He couldn't elicit a clear response, but it was clear there was no testing material and the immunotherapy would continue blindly. Dad wasn't happy. This particular treatment was costing the family £12,000; he felt conned and there was nothing for it but to hope that the vaccine would work. He was not confident.

By the end of the first month, Mum was trying hard to envisage just how much George's condition had deteriorated. Dad, however, was now worrying about how George would make the journey home. When he spoke to a senior person in the hospital, voicing his concern, he was told bluntly that he would have to organise a stretcher for the flights home. Accordingly, they investigated the provision of a stretcher for the long flight from Hong Kong and were informed by Cathay Pacific that the charge would be thirteen thousand pounds: they simply couldn't afford it. Next, they attempted to upgrade to first class, but there were no seats available. George would simply have to rely on morphine and painkiller injections to get him through and hope that he could sleep through the worst of it. Mum was terrified that they would be stuck in China.

---o---

Mum was due to journey to Sheffield for her PhD viva. The night before the exam, she received the news that her aunt – her godmother – had died. Mum felt heavy and unmotivated to make the trip to attend her examination. Her aunt had been deteriorating fast over the past few weeks. She lived alone in sheltered housing, had no children and relied mostly on a neighbour from her previous address to help her out. Mum was sad and wished she could have done more to help, but she was too caught up in what was happening to George. Somehow, though, she would have to get to Hertfordshire for the funeral.

Despite this, the next day Mum set off for the University of Sheffield. At least she felt confident about all the work she had put in. As it happened, she was able to say afterwards that she found it an enjoyable experience. The examiners seemed genuinely interested in her work. They watched the film of a dance that had been made as part of her research, by a male performer labelled as having learning difficulties. He communicated his deepest thoughts and feelings, achieving levels of sophistication in thought that he would have struggled to achieve in words. Mum was fascinated by this ability to 'think through the body'.

Before the viva she had lunch with her PhD supervisor. When they had finished discussing the pending exam, they chatted about things in general. Although her supervisor looked well, she had had a tough time. Some months previously she had begun suffering seizures, which turned out to be the result of a head injury from a car accident a couple of years before. She had two young children, one of whom was disabled, had been through a divorce and was holding down a demanding job. Yet, here she was, looking great, smiling and full of energy and encouragement for Mum. She was quite a remarkable woman, Mum thought. Yes, it was amazing what people could learn to cope with.

After the viva, Mum returned on the train to London Kings Cross and finally arrived back in South West London, pleased but weary, to pick Louis up from Max's at 10 p.m. Louis was very congratulatory and she was formally christened 'Dr Mum', to go alongside 'Dr Dad'. She was desperate to talk to Panik and share her success with him and she stayed up late to try and reach him on Skype, but without success. She felt let down, upset and angry that he hadn't made the effort to contact her and ask how it had gone. Finally she went to bed totally miserable. It wasn't until late the next morning that she finally spoke to Panik. All her anger melted away immediately. He was beside himself with worry; things were not going well. George was having a hard time; he was in considerable pain, had been put on more morphine, was nauseous and had lost his appetite.

The truth was that George was now very ill. Between the tumour on the pelvis and the treatment he was having, he was becoming thinner and weaker every day and his mobility was diminishing. Neither was he in a good state mentally; the pain and suffering were beginning to take their toll. Mum and Dad began to worry that he wouldn't be able to make the journey home and would end up staying in China until he died. They began counting the days – the hours – to the return journey.

---o---

Mum, Louis and Despina decided to spruce up George's bedroom as a home-coming surprise. They knew he had wanted a sofa in his room and so Mum went to Ikea with her friend Carine and picked up a nice blue check sofa bed, to fit in with his blue and aqua colour scheme. Carine and her husband put it together on the Sunday before George was due back, while Despina and Mum looked on in awe at their efficiency, feeling a little bit stupid at their own inadequacy in this area, demoted to the role of cushion cover stuffers. Then Louis, Despina and Mum set about cleaning, scrubbing and rearranging George's room and putting up posters – including a four-foot-wide picture of the moon shining on the sea at night, which had been bought by Auntie Ann. This they placed on the wall opposite George's bed. They tidied up and placed an artificial blue rose in a tall, blue vase on top of his chest of drawers, along with various other bits and pieces. The whole effect was bright and pleasing and they were quite excited in anticipation of George's reaction to their surprise.

They had all worked extremely hard, but there was one more job they wanted to do if they could manage it. George had been given a table football game by his uncle, but it had been sitting in its box, behind the door for almost a year. While Louis went off to play his own football match, Despina and Mum set to putting it together. Three hours later, weary and a little short-tempered from the effort of fixing the many awkward – and at times ill-fitting – parts together, they had finished. Then Louis arrived home and pointed out that they had put the goals on back to front. He was not popular! Mum and Despina set silently about righting their mistake, jaws set in determination to get the damned thing up. At last it was finished. Mum thought it was probably the most cooperative her and Despina had ever been with each other, united in a common goal for George's sake. Louis thought they would have been nowhere without him. Later, George was to comment that they had put the crossbars, which held the players, in the wrong order.

"Everyone's a critic!" thought Mum.

---o---

Back in China, Dad and George were dreading the journey home. George had been trying to build his strength by taking short walks in the corridor and practising getting in and out of a wheelchair, but progress was slow. He was always in pain and his leg was showing no sign of improvement. The doctors were insisting that the leg was merely suffering from local inflammation after the cryoablation, but George was rightly convinced that the damage to the nerve was permanent. His primary concern was still that it would be impossible for him to continue with his driving lessons – one of the few things that had kept him going through the hard times.

Finally, early evening on Saturday 10th November, after more than five weeks in China, George and Dad left Fuda, along with several other patients. George was given a final injection of prednisolone into his back, which was expected to act as a pain block for 24 hours – enough time to complete the journey home, with a couple of hours to spare. In addition, Dad had been given some back-up pills. While they waited for the bus to arrive to take them to the airport, Dad was on edge, terrified about what lay ahead. George was installed in a wheelchair, but when the time came, getting him out of the wheelchair and onto the bus was slow and painful. When finally he was settled as comfortably as could be managed, there followed what seemed an interminable wait, while a whole batch of patients were collected from different parts of the hospital. Fortunately, the first leg of the journey – back through the city – was calm. George was still attempting to take photos, but without much success this time.

The party of patients was accompanied by a translator, but it was George and Dad who took up most of his time, as George was unable to wait in line to check in or to board without help. At the check-in desk the translator requested an airport wheelchair and a porter, but once George had been transferred to the new wheelchair, the translator left and they were on their own once again, waiting anxiously for the porter to arrive. Eventually he came and they were suddenly whisked through customs, sailing past endless long queues of bored and frustrated looking travellers. They joked that it was the only way to travel, but in reality every little bump and knock caused George to wince. And at security he was forced to get out of his chair and inch his way through the barrier to take a seat in yet another wheelchair that stood waiting for him on the other side.

Finally, they boarded the flight from Guangzhou to Hong Kong. On the plane they were situated in one of the three-seat sections, but luckily a sympathetic steward steered other passengers away from the spare seat, giving George a little extra space. The two travellers tried to relax a little, but all they could think about was the long flight from Hong Kong to London that lay ahead.

At Hong Kong they were thrown into panic when once again their flight was cancelled. Chaos ensued, as staff in their red, Cathay Pacific uniforms ran around trying to sort things out. George was shuttled from one side of the airport to the other in a bumpy old wheelchair pushed by a porter clearly more interested in breaking speed records than anything else and who ignored their repeated requests to be more careful. The sight they beheld at the boarding gate was not encouraging either. There was a huge crush of about two hundred people all demanding attention at once. Dad steeled himself, left George on the periphery and began to push and shove his way through, ignoring the protests of other angry passengers. He made it through the crowd, but had to speak to several of the airline staff before he could find one that would listen properly. He explained forcefully that George was seriously ill and something needed to be done for him. Eventually, it was announced that people would be billeted in different hotels and, along with one or two other elderly or sick passengers, Dad and George were allotted a fancy hotel attached to the airport, where they were duly taken, along with all their luggage.

A sense of unreality kicked in when they were faced with a hotel that looked like something out of a Hollywood movie. Their room, high above the city, offered a view that was easily equal to that which could be seen from Fuda's rooftop. Clad in dark-brown wood panelling that was actually rather staid-looking, it was seriously impressive and luxurious. The twin beds were covered in sumptuous satin covers, and thick white bathrobes and towels were supplied in the all-white bathroom. They revealed their lowly backgrounds when George set about pocketing the pens and notelets, while Dad collected up all of the soaps. But it was now well after midnight and they had no more energy to appreciate their exotic surroundings. They were already exhausted, were still only in Hong Kong and had to be up at 5.30 a.m. ready to leave. Dad was worried that the prednisolone would wear off before they reached home and he also needed to contact Mum to let her know what had happened. They were unable to enjoy the luxury they had unexpectedly found themselves in and instead, after Dad had sent a text to Mum, went straight to bed.

---o---

Thousands of miles away at home, where it was still Wednesday, the countdown to their arrival was making Mum, Louis and Despina tense. Everyone was worried about George on the journey; Mum was worrying about Dad; the waiting was unbearable. And when she received the text from Dad to say they were delayed in Hong Kong, her anxiety level doubled. What if the pain relief wore off? What if George simply couldn't manage to board the plane to London? What if they had to turn back and they were stuck in China? What if? What if? Louis made Mum laugh though, when he said he dreamt that Dad and George came back looking Chinese. She said that the Duke of Edinburgh would probably put it down to the food.

Mum and Louis cleaned the house, walked the

dog and planned the journey to Heathrow. That was also the day Mum learnt that she was to inherit several thousand pounds from her aunt. It was a strange feeling to be profiting from someone else's death – something she had never experienced before. She tried not to think about what she would do with the money. Anyway, it would take a long time to go through probate etc.

---o---

In Hong Kong it was morning, but there was no time to take advantage of the fancy breakfast on offer at the hotel. A porter arrived with a wheel-chair and they were on their way once again. At the airport everything seemed to take forever. George sat quietly, clearly in pain, and Dad was silent beside him. They had run out of small talk and were simply desperate to get home. On the plane, Dad began to feed the additional painkillers to George at the allotted times, but he was secretly worried that even this supply would run out before they arrived home. What would George do then? At least the plane turned out to be more comfortable for George than they had anticipated. Or was it simply that he was past complaining? They settled down to watch a couple of films in a somewhat desultory fashion because their hearts were not really in it. They ate whatever they were given and waited until everyone was asleep before attempting to manoeuvre George out of his seat and down the aisle to the cramped toilet. Then, back in their seats, they drifted into a restless, light sleep.

Whenever he was conscious, and even in his sleep sometimes, Dad was tortured by the thought that they were making this journey for George to return home to die. It was a horrible thought, but it wouldn't go away. The truth was that all hope had now been extinguished for Dad, and all he was left with was exhaustion and sadness and the sorrow of knowing that his lovely boy had no chances left. It didn't mean that they wouldn't carry on searching. He still hoped that he could find some other treatment, something that would help George to keep the cancer under control, that might extend his life long enough for a cure to be found perhaps. But deep down, as he drifted in and out of sleep, he knew he was clutching at straws.

---o---

At last, the day arrived for Mum and Louis. It was Thursday 11th November 2010 and the flight was due into Heathrow at 1.30 p.m., assuming there had been no further delays. Mum and Louis drove to the airport around midday; Despina was working and extremely upset that she couldn't get time off to come to the airport, or be there to see George's face when he saw the improvements to his bedroom. She would have to be content with coming round later that evening.

At the airport Mum parked the car and they took the lift up to arrivals to stand alongside the many people searching the display monitors for landing details. As they waited for the flight to arrive, they bought some sandwiches and sat down to eat them on the seats at the edge of the big arrivals hall. They watched the many passengers arriving, who, sun-tanned and relaxed, if a little tired, emerged with luggage trolleys piled high, greeting family and friends with sometimes passionate embraces. They noted the usual taxi drivers and individuals working for the corporate sector, standing around holding up names on pieces of card.

---o---

Back on the plane, once it had landed, Dad and George, so desperate to be home, had to wait while everyone else disembarked. The stewardesses made a fuss of them though. They were invited to sit in the first class compartment while they waited for a wheelchair to arrive, and they were astounded to hear the cost of a first class ticket from Hong Kong to Heathrow. George of course was impressed with the bling of it and, as he sat smiling and joking, Dad briefly glimpsed the old George again – eyes alive, laughing, wise-cracking and enjoying the moment.

---o---

When Mum and Louis saw that the flight from Hong Kong had finally landed it seemed an age before baggage was 'in hall', but at last they took their places amongst the many other people at the barrier, anticipating the imminent arrival of Dad and George. Dad had organised a wheelchair and disability assistance for George, and finally Louis spotted him being wheeled out. Mum let out a cry and they both ran to greet the weary travellers. They hugged and kissed and Louis held on tight to his dad. Mum saw with dismay how much thinner and paler George had become.

When they reached the car Dad set about helping George into the back seat, as he couldn't lift his leg or manoeuvre at all easily. Trying to swivel himself round into the car seat was painful, despite the seats of the Zafira being quite high off the ground, and it took several attempts before he was properly installed. For Dad, a feeling of unreality overtook him. As they drove home through torrential rain, he noted that such a downpour wouldn't have been out of place in tropical Guangzhou, except that it was much colder in England. They passed an accident outside the airport, where a young man had managed to crash his car in such a way that the whole engine was lying in the road next to it. He seemed unhurt, just a little bewildered and worried. They laughed and joked as they envisaged him trying to explain to his parents that there was a bit of a problem with their car that he'd borrowed. It was all silliness, but it helped to ease the tension.

On the way home though, George was in increasing amounts of pain from the mounting pressure on his pelvis and the last five minutes of the journey were fraught with tension and worry, as his cries of pain grew in frequency and volume. Mum was shocked by the deterioration in his condition. Little did they know that some weeks later they would experience a much worse car journey that would end all possibility of George travelling by car ever again.

At home at last, Flash ran to greet them, wagging his tail madly at the sight of George. In the end, they had to pull him away so that the boy could climb the stairs slowly to his room. Mum made some apology about his room being a bit of a mess, as they hadn't had time to clean it.

George said, "No matter" and Louis stifled a laugh.

He ran to open the door for George, who stepped in and let out a "wow!"

The hard work had been worth it; he was genuinely surprised and pleased. They settled him down on his bed and he admired their handiwork. He was pale, thin, fragile and more than a little relieved to be home. Mum left him to settle in and set about making fish chowder and some garlic bread, which she knew he liked.

In the evening, Despina arrived, full of anticipation at seeing her brother and Dad again, but the sight of George lying in bed with Dad sitting next to him, both of them looking pale and exhausted, frightened her. Dad's eyes were bloodshot from the tiredness, but George – so gaunt, so fragile – looked to her like a victim of a concentration camp. She sat with him and Louis, watching a DVD and chatting, but she couldn't see how he would recover from this; that night, back in her flat, she cried herself to sleep.

That evening, Mum and Dad discussed things over a glass of good merlot – Dad's favourite. He had been teetotal in China and now he savoured every mouthful of the mellow, fruity liquid as he lay back against the cushions on the sofa. He was pale and exhausted – from travelling, from worry, from fear. But he was so relieved that they were finally home again and for a while he sobbed like a baby in Mum's arms.

All the while, they were both asking themselves,

"What happens next?"

14. Home Again and Poorly

George settled into being home, but he was never to be the same again. He stayed mostly in his room, as the effort to climb up and down the stairs was too much for him. His posts on Facebook had diminished, although friends still contacted him. He would spend long hours lying in bed, arising only to make the trip to the hospital or to play on his Xbox for a while, or sit on his new sofa when Mum and Dad could persuade him to. He found all chairs uncomfortable now. Mum adapted a fold-up beach chair, padding it out with a quilted cover, and he found this bearable for a while. It was suggested that they might put his bed in the sitting room, but Mum and Dad were reluctant to do this: he had all his possessions around him in his room and the sitting room was the only comfortable sitting space in the house for other people to use. In the end, visitors went upstairs to George's room and sat on his sofa to chat to him. Sometimes huge contingents of the family would arrive and install themselves in his bedroom, perched on the sofa and various chairs –

Despina, Yiayia, Buppou, Uncle David, Auntie Ann and cousins Zoe and Sofia, or Auntie Barb, Auntie Flo with cousins Dimitri and Luca. Cousin Nikki would occasionally come down from university in Manchester and sit and chat. Cousin Penny, already out at work, would come over independently to visit him. Then there was George's best friend, who popped in sometimes. It was hard to see the distress on the young man's face, as he saw how much his friend was deteriorating.

It was now clear that the treatments in China hadn't killed the tumour in the pelvis. Despite probably having wiped out a large percentage of the cells (it was hard to be accurate from the scans), the cancer was still growing and spreading. Dad was convinced that the immunotherapy in particular had been a waste of a considerable sum of money. Mum and Dad both knew that George was in a worse state than before he left for China; everyone knew it, including George. It was hard to take. Dad would angst over it time and again, blaming himself for taking George. Mum would repeat over and over again that he did what any parent would do under the circumstances and that George had wanted to go. What else should they have done? If they had stayed in England, what would have happened? The tumour would have grown unchecked and perhaps George would have been in a worse state by now. But later, as his suffering increased, George himself was to regret having made the trip.

In the meantime he was finding it hard to keep his food down. In the days that followed his return, Mum would make all the food she could think of to tempt him, but he would eat only a small amount and struggle against vomiting. It was hard to watch the boy, who had taken such delight in food, lose all the pleasure eating had once afforded him. They began to worry about his weight loss; it really did appear that he could be starving to death if they didn't do something fast.

During a visit to the Marsden the following week he was given various build-up drinks, plus advice on how to increase the calories in food by adding cream etc. The glucose in the drinks gave Mum and Dad the creeps, as they envisaged the tumour sucking it all up, but George needed some sustenance, given that he could barely keep any solid food down and he was keen to try the drinks. He was now officially under the palliative care team, for management of pain and other symptoms of the disease. He was prescribed oral opiate-based painkillers and a type of lollipop painkiller, to be sucked for fairly instant pain relief when acute attacks were hard to handle, such as when travelling by car. Ironically, waiting around for his medication to be sorted by the hospital pharmacy caused him considerable amounts of pain. As the weeks passed, he could no longer tolerate either being on his feet or sitting for more than ten minutes at a time.

Visits to the Marsden had a different feel now. As soon as they arrived, it was important to identify a bed for George to lie down on, as the level of pain he was experiencing meant that he couldn't sit for long periods in Day Care's waiting area. The focus was on keeping him comfortable; there was no more talk of curative treatments. And George was focused mostly on dealing with the pain.

Not long after Dad and George returned from China, Mum went alone to her aunt's funeral. She met up with cousins, who had thankfully taken care of all the arrangements. They spent a half-hour or so at their aunt's flat, taking a trip down memory lane, looking at old family photos and Mum picked out a couple of mementos. At the crematorium chapel a small crowd of friends and neighbours joined them for the service. Mum sat with her cousins, watching a ladybird walking backwards and forwards for the duration of the ceremony, along the back of the empty pew in front.

"That's Aunt Rene," they said, "come to watch."

Mum kept thinking, "It will be George next."

She baulked at the religious platitudes expressed by the vicar, and seethed with anger at the idea of a god who would let a poor boy suffer so much. What lengths people would go to justify it! After the ceremony there was a reception in a small hotel. It was good to catch up with family that she hadn't seen for years – just a pity it was always at funerals these days.

Back home, a week later George had an appointment with a physiotherapist at the Marsden. Mum and Dad were desperate to get some advice for their son about manoeuvring himself in and out of bed, as well as learning exercises to relieve some of the stiffness and help build some strength in his frail frame. In the midst of all this George was still concerned about his driving lessons; he had by no means given up on learning to drive. His other aim was to be able to go to Kingston with Despina and Louis, for a coffee. At present he was completely unable to cope with the ten-minute bus ride or the twenty-minute walk with crutches. He was given a wheelchair, but wasn't keen to use it. Apart from the stigma he felt, it was not actually comfortable and caused just as much pain in his pelvis as on all but the flattest of surfaces.

The appointment to see the physiotherapist was scheduled for the afternoon and Mum, Dad and George set off in the car after lunch. It was a wintry day and the weather forecast had predicted snow, although it was coming down only lightly in the Kingston area. However, it seemed that it might become worse in Sutton, where the Marsden was situated. The traffic was heavy; George was nervous. Mum rang the physiotherapist and explained that they would be late. The physio suggested they cancel, as the weather was worsening and some members of staff were already leaving early as a precaution. Mum and Dad, concerned about George's deteriorating condition, were keen to see her and so they pushed on.

As the snow began to fall more heavily, George requested outright that they turn round and go home, but the parents were set on getting there somehow and they carried on. George was not happy. They continued to make slow progress for a while, until finally even Mum and Dad could see it would be better to think about turning back. Then suddenly, just as the decision was made, it was too late. The snow came falling down thick and fast and the traffic slowed to a halt; they were stuck.

After a while they began to crawl along at a snail's pace. They were still only half way to the Marsden and George was in pain. They finally managed to turn round, but by then it was too late. The traffic in the opposite direction was also creeping along and cars were beginning to skid, as the thick layer of snow on the road was compressed by the wheels of a slow, but endless, stream of vehicles.

From then on it was like a living nightmare. George was moaning in the back-seat, as his pain level increased, until he could cope no longer. He took various doses of pain relief and used the painkiller lollipop, but the pain was still intensifying. To make matters worse, he was unable to manoeuvre himself into a more comfortable position; even moving an inch was agony. In fact, it became clear that there was no comfortable position for him in the car any more and now he was completely stuck with the pain level still rising.

Mum rang the palliative care team, who offered advice in terms of how much they could increase the dose, but the tablets took up to an hour to kick in fully. There was nothing else to do, but get home as soon as possible.

George sat in the back of the car crying and pleading "Help me, please help me."

But Mum and Dad could do nothing to help; and they knew they were responsible for putting him through this. They should have listened to him, not pushed on, putting their own agenda first. They sat helplessly in the front of the car, trying in vain to calm George down, while he sat and begged for the help they couldn't give.

By the time they finally arrived home, they had been driving around for three hours and hadn't even made it to the hospital. George never travelled by car again.

At this point George was still able to get in and out of bed with some help to lift the leg with the damaged nerve. If the timing was misjudged the pain to his pelvis was excruciating. At night he had found a way of getting back into bed by himself, with considerable effort, by sliding himself up from the foot of the bed. He did this in order not to rouse Dad, who was still going into work when he could and was becoming increasingly exhausted from lack of sleep. Mum had asked if he could manage alone – as Dad always woke up, even if someone else helped George – and he had obligingly found a way. Then one night George fell.

Mum and Dad were woken by a crash and a cry; they shot out of bed and into George's room. He was lying, collapsed and groaning with pain, against the radiator under the window. He had been out to the toilet, and although he had used his crutch, he had pivoted on it and slipped on the way back to bed and fallen. On the way down he had caught his finger on something; it was cut nastily on top, near the nail, was bleeding profusely and already bruising black. He was in agony from his hip and Mum and Dad were terrified he might have fractured his now fragile pelvis. It was awful to see him there, helpless, bleeding and in pain.

After a minute of checking to see the extent of the damage, they all three began negotiating a strategy to get him back on his feet. Dad bit the bullet, took George's arm and instructed Mum to take the other and pull him slowly to his feet. Mum was afraid of the pain it would cause, but Dad insisted they get on with it quickly, as it was the only way they were going to get him up. George cried out as he rose to his feet, but they were able to then get him successfully back into bed. It was all too horrible for words. Dad insisted that from then on he would get up to help George at all times. If only they had known how much worse it was going to get.

A week after the snow incident, on Wednesday December 8th, George went by ambulance to the Marsden for an MRI scan of his head, neck and pelvis, plus an X-ray of his abdomen. The results the following week confirmed a large soft tissue mass extending out from the already diseased pelvic bone, and a soft tissue mass in his throat. In addition, George's knee was swollen and there was pain in his thigh.

The day after they received the MRI results, George was taken to Kingston Hospital by ambulance. Although his right knee had been slightly swollen for a while, it was now surrounded by red blotches and the whole leg had swelled up – from the top of his thigh down to his ankle. It was painful and he was terrified that he had developed a deep vein thrombosis (DVT). It was late at night when he and Dad arrived at Kingston and after some initial examinations, the doctors still weren't sure what was going on in the leg. It looked like a DVT, but there would need to be an X-ray and an ultrasound scan to confirm this, neither of which could be done before morning. The next day, investigations did indeed confirm that George had suffered an acute DVT, but he was assured that as long as it was controlled with a prescription of fragmin – to prevent blood clotting – he would be ok. He came home a little relieved, if somewhat tired and not exactly happy.

A week later, the leg was still swelling badly and George was once again taken to Kingston Hospital on Tuesday 21st December. Again it was late at night and very little could happen at that point. It was clear that he and Dad would need to stay the night once again but, although they were by this time more than ready to bed down, there was a problem – the room they had been assigned was not meant for overnight stays, and there were no over-night beds available. Actually, there were lots of beds and empty rooms, but Dad was told that the rules forbade their use because there weren't enough nurses to cover them. Father and son pleaded that they didn't need to be looked after, they just needed somewhere to sleep, but all to no avail. Consequently, they had to wait until the early hours of the morning for an ambulance to transport them from Kingston to the Marsden. It was a painful journey, with every bump in the road causing George to wince. Finally, arriving at the Marsden, they found there was no bed available in the children's ward and so George was admitted to an adult ward, where he didn't know the staff and they weren't used to dealing with young people. He was less than happy. All in all, it was another exhausting few days for the family.

During this time, while attending an appointment

at the Marsden, George was started on a treatment of zoledronic acid, given by infusion. Dad had wanted George to have this from very early on, before the disease had metastasised, as it had been shown to have some anti-cancer effect in bone tumours, but it had been refused. The palliative care team were now willing to give it only on the basis that it had been shown to bring some relief from cancer pain in the bones. In addition, a week later, their oncologist prescribed oral chemotherapy to try and help slow down the tumour growth, in order to keep George comfortable for as long as possible. The pelvic tumour was now highly visible as a large mass on George's hip and he was aware of a feeling of considerable pressure caused by it, as well as the stiffness felt in his leg from the water-retention swelling caused by the DVT.

At home, George spent less and less time getting out of his bed. When he had first returned from China, he had passed some time each day sitting in his chair, playing on his Xbox. But gradually, the effort of sitting, with the discomfort it caused, became too much for him. He was confined to bed more and more.

By mid-December the palliative care team were carrying out home visits on a weekly basis and were contactable by telephone any hour of the day or night. They were headed by a consultant called Melanie – a large friendly, cheerful New Zealander, with short, blonde hair and a fun dress sense. She would often turn up in a brightly-coloured, flared, short skirt and Flash would make a point of shoving his snout up it as a greeting. Melanie would sit at George's bedside and talk quietly to him about how he was feeling, how he was dealing with the pain and what she could do to help make his life more comfortable.

In addition, the PONT, who had been responsible for changing dressings to wounds, were now visiting every day to check on medication and help with washing etc. They were also on 24-hour call. They were a godsend. They came with a smile, with reassurance, a sympathetic ear and plenty of jokes and banter. As the weeks passed, Mum looked forward to their visits – as a part of daily routine, a safety net, a support in dealing with the unknown. She would ply them with homemade rice pudding or rhubarb crumble and cups of tea, and in return knew that they would be there at any hour of the day or night to support unexpected events. They looked after the family as much as they cared for George, and Mum and Dad could not have coped without them.

---o---

And so the long days passed. Each morning George would wake at around 10.30, lifting his heavy-lidded eyes to greet yet another day of the same boring routine, trapped in his bed. He would manoeuvre himself to a sitting position, propped up on his pillows, and set about the business of trying to keep his breakfast down. Then he would swallow the increasing number of pills handed to him by Mum or Dad, and clean what remained of his teeth with his electric toothbrush, spitting carefully into the bowl placed under his chin. Two nurses from the PONT would arrive to change the fentanyl pain relief patches on his arm and maybe give him a good wash and change his sheets, working slowly and methodically with George, turning him carefully on to either side in turn to complete their task. If necessary, they would ring the palliative care team doctors to discuss raising the different pain relief doses. By the time they left, George would often be exhausted and doze for a couple of hours. If not, he would watch a DVD or some TV, before attempting a small amount of lunch – a soft omelette, or a child's portion of pasta. Mum and Dad would wait anxiously to see if the food would stay down. Sometimes George was lucky, but often there would be some vomiting within an hour or two. Visitors would arrive mid to late afternoon. All the while, Dad, who was working from home on his laptop most of the time now, would sit with George. Later in the day Despina would arrive to spend time with her brother. After dinner there would be more vomiting from George. Dying of cancer was a tedious, messy business.

By now, it had been established that George's nausea and sickness was most certainly caused by an acute blockage of the gut from faecal impaction that had been building up since he'd first been started on opiate-based painkillers in China. Dad later discovered that there was a drug called methylnaltrexone, which could have been given alongside the opiates to prevent this occurrence. But although this drug was in widespread use in the USA and other countries, it was not often used in the UK and wasn't prescribed to George. He was, however, prescribed high levels of laxatives, which caused additional pain and discomfort. Soon he was to suffer the indignity of enemas and being cleaned up by the nurses or even his parents when accidents occurred. George was bedridden, constantly tired, beginning to suffer headaches and starting to feel spaced out. It was hard to tell how much it was the drugs affecting him and how much it was the cancer. The tumour at the back of his throat was perilously close to his brain and probably growing in that direction. The prognosis was extremely grim.

Meanwhile, as George became more poorly, the weather continued to get colder. More snow was forecast for the weekend before Christmas, when Mum and Louis were to visit Nanny Olive for a few days (in between the two visits to Kingston Hospital for George's swollen leg). The family would obviously not be going to Southwold this year for their usual New Year stay and Mum wanted to see her mother before Christmas. However, on the morning she and Louis were to leave, snow was forecast to begin falling late morning, gradually spreading up from Kent. Mum calculated that they could stay just ahead of it on the journey. Unfortunately, the snow started falling before they left, but despite Dad's protests, albeit with a certain feeling of trepidation, Mum set off with Louis.

After only twenty minutes of driving, and even before they reached the motorway, the roads were thick with snow. When they pulled on to the M25, vehicles were creeping along encased in a world of white. The snow was falling heavily and, as the wipers struggled to push it away, the windscreen soon became clogged with ice around the edges. Gradually this encroached more and more on Mum's area of vision, until she could see through only a very small patch of the glass. At this point, it was necessary to wind down the window, reach round to the front with a scraper and clear as much of the build-up as possible. All would be well for fifteen minutes when the process would have to be repeated.

Travelling at 10 to 15 miles per hour, they began passing a number of cars skidding round in circles and grinding to a halt. They were amused to discover that these vehicles were all BMWs. Not so amusing was the need to navigate around any vehicle blocking the way, without sliding on the same patch of ice. Then they came across a large truck stretched almost across the whole width of the three-lane motorway. The entire road had turned into a vast, white obstacle course; drivers had long abandoned any attempt to work out where the lanes were and simply resorted to following the car in front and navigating around the ice in whatever way they could best manage.

Where the motorway divided at junction five, they came to a complete standstill and here they stayed for about forty-five minutes. Mum was desperate to pee, but there was only one bush in sight. It was occupied by a man who had shouted at her when she had pulled back on to the road after the one and only time she had skidded. She told Louis she wasn't about to doubly humiliate herself by going and peeing in front of him. Louis laughed. But as soon as the man had finished she swallowed her pride and shot over to the bush. Luckily the traffic started moving again soon after.

The journey continued in much the same fashion for several hours, when they were able to stop for tea and sandwiches before continuing on. In all, it took them nine hours to reach Nanny Olive's – a journey that normally lasted three. Louis had been fantastic the whole time – uncomplaining, calm, supportive and generally good company. Luckily, the journey home three days later went smoothly, as the snow had almost all melted, and they arrived back a couple of days before Christmas.Meanwhile, back at home George was in much the same state as when they had left, except that his leg was continuing to swell, which would provoke the second visit to Kingston Hospital. His days were still tediously long and peppered with bouts of increased pain and discomfort. He was still vomiting after food and sleeping increasing amounts. Visitors relieved the boredom, but on occasions, when he felt too low, he would refuse to allow them to come – apart from his sister, who being part of the immediate family, he was always very pleased to see, no matter what state he was in.

Christmas was looming, but it was not going to be the usual family affair. Given George's deteriorating condition, his increasing level of pain, his immobility and inability to keep his food down, it was not even clear if he would manage to keep out of hospital. The family viewed the holiday with some trepidation.

For The Love of George

15. The Hardest Thing

In the days leading up to Christmas, George mentioned to Despina that he wished he could see the Christmas tree downstairs. And so when Despina said she would decorate his room, he gave her a list of things he wanted and she went off to Kingston to duly purchase them. When she returned she spent a couple of hours decking his room out with Christmas lights and tinsel; he was pleased with the results. Then she helped him wrap his presents, as he was now having trouble using his hands for delicate operations. She was doing her best to help him get into the Christmas spirit.

Christmas Eve arrived. Along with it came a visit from the symptoms care team. Melanie and colleague arrived mid-morning, as two nurses from the PONT had just finished washing George. When Melanie entered Dad saw that she was carrying 'the box'; his stomach turned over.

Dad had already told Mum about 'the box'. He was aware of it from a discussion on the children's ward at the Marsden. It was a large plain plastic box – like a fancy toolbox with cantilevered shelves and lots of compartments – with a chunky padlock and it contained emergency medication, including sedatives and very strong pain-killers. The box was delivered to the home when a cancer patient was dying. George's box had arrived. From now on, the box would live at the house, although only the nurses would know the combination of the lock.

Mum and Dad showed the nurses and doctors into the sitting room and then made tea for everyone. They chatted lightly about nothing in particular, but in the back of their minds they dreaded the conversation they knew was to come.

When they were all sitting down, Dad asked finally, "How long?"

The reply was delivered quietly by Melanie, "Maybe a couple of weeks, maybe less."

They cried; the nurses comforted them. Then they all went upstairs to see George. No one mentioned the box or its implications.

George smiled weakly as everyone entered his room and admired the purple and silver colour scheme of his Christmas decorations. Melanie sat by his bed and talked quietly, asking the usual questions about pain level and sickness. George focused on the issues in his usual quiet manner. Yes, the tumour pain was mostly under control, but there was still breakthrough pain at least once a day. The DVT swelling was still bothering him and giving him bouts of pain, but Mum, Dad and Despina were taking it in turns to manipulate his ankle as they had been taught, to try and help with drainage. Yes, he was attempting the exercises the physio had shown him when she had visited. He was managing to keep some food down and the enemas were helping now. They discussed increasing the dosage of the pain medications and then Melanie and colleague left, wishing him a Merry Christmas with cheery smiles that belied the seriousness of the situation. A little later the PONT also left.

Dad went to sit with George. Mum went down to start the festive cooking and called Louis – who hadn't been party to the earlier discussion – to join her. Somehow they would have to break it gently to the younger boy and his sister that their brother might not have long. It was going to be a very hard Christmas – even harder than they had anticipated – but they were desperate to give George a good day. Somehow they had to get through Christmas Day. It seemed of the utmost importance that he shouldn't die on that day of all days. His death would be devastating on any day, but to die on Christmas Day…

And so, on Christmas morning, after breakfast, when George was fully awake, Dad, Mum, Despina and Louis ascended to George's room, loaded down with carrier bags full of presents. Christmas this year would be held in George's room and it would begin with present opening.

George, propped up on pillows, was handed his presents one by one from a considerable pile. With a little assistance, he managed to open and appreciate them all.

There were many lovely gifts, including a special artist's easel for using in bed from Despina, a box-set of the Madagascar DVDs from Louis (George was spending a lot of time watching old cartoons with Despina), a new poster of a large, deep blue flower from Mum and Dad, clothes, chocolates, a parcel from the local children's hospice and many more. Mum and Dad had bought a blue lava lamp from Nanny Olive and from then on it became a nightly ritual to switch on the lamp and watch the globules of wax melt from the cold, twisted, alien sculptures – that sometimes looked like strange foetuses in a medical jar – into soft, floating blobs of hot blue oil. They were always on the lookout for things that might help relax George, help pass the time, remind him of the things he wanted to do – like his art.

George, who had done his Christmas shopping on the Internet, had bought Mum a burner for essential oils. However, it was to remain in George's room thereafter, burning eucalyptus oil to help him breathe, or orange oil, to cover the smell of sickness and the smell of his body breaking down. The smell of sickness and death was never to leave his bedroom, even years later, as if it was woven into the very fabric of the room itself. They always kept a window open and would burn the sweet orange oil and switch the lava lamp on as dusk came.

By the end of present opening time, George's bed was covered in wrapping paper and on the floor was a huge pile of gifts. They cleared up and, while Mum and Dad went downstairs to prepare lunch, he spent the morning dozing and watching a film with his brother and sister. The PONT nurses would arrive later.

At 2.00 p.m. Christmas lunch was served and they all sat once again on the sofa and chairs in George's room, their plates piled high with turkey, stuffing, cranberry sauce, 'pigs in blankets', roast parsnips, carrots, broccoli, gravy. George had demanded a whole turkey leg and it covered most of his plate. They wondered if he would really be able to eat it, but he sat and gnawed slowly in his quietly determined way through a great part of it. It was good to see him being able to eat one of his favourite foods and enjoy it, despite his weak state and shortage of teeth.

Two hours later George was being sick. They tried to tell themselves that, despite this, he had enjoyed the meal and they had succeeded in getting through the main events of Christmas Day. It would have been terrible if he had been unable to participate at all or had slipped away from them before it was over. As it was, Christmas was never going to be the same again, but they knew things could have been worse and they were grateful for small mercies.

On Boxing Day things did get worse: George's condition deteriorated considerably. He was unable to keep any food down, stopped eating completely and was barely drinking. He suffered a severe migraine pain on his right eye, which Mum, Dad and Despina tried desperately to relieve for him. They drew the curtains, applied soothing cooling gel, gently massaged him, gave him pain relief, but all to no avail. That day, pain relief was switched from oral intake to infusion. The next day, a catheter was inserted. George had become light and sound sensitive and was spending most of the time in a deep sleep, with the curtains drawn and the lights off.

Dad, Mum and Despina took it in turns to do one-and-a-half hour watches, sitting by George's bed in the dark. Despina often sat longer, so that Mum could prepare food or Dad could have a rest. It was a strange experience, sitting in his room in the dark, with only the sound of George's often irregular, rasping breathing. The curtains were drawn and it was very cold, as the radiators were turned off because George couldn't stand the heat. Despina would wrap herself in a blanket to try and keep warm; Mum would don an extra jumper. If they wanted to give him a sip of drink, when he occasionally roused himself, they had to use a torch to find the cup and straw, taking care not to shine it near George. From time to time, someone would come in with a welcome cup of hot tea for the person on duty.

When she wasn't with George, Mum would prepare food for them to eat in shifts. The house was quiet, there was already an air of grieving – which is exactly what they were all doing. They were in expectation of his imminent death and already mourning for the loss of him. At the same time, in the background there were the usual family Christmas happenings – the watching of a new DVD, listening to a new CD, petty little squabbles, especially between Mum and Despina, but everything was dampened by the enormity of the situation.

When she was with George, Mum spent her time

with her eyes closed, concentrating very hard and trying to communicate with George somehow telepathically. It was a bizarre thing to do and probably served more as an antidote to the impotence she felt than anything else. She tried to imagine she was inside George's head and she spoke to him there. She imagined, there inside him, the innocent little curly-haired boy she had once known, riding around on his tricycle with his cheeky grin, and she spoke to him. She told the grown up George that it was ok to let go if he had had enough. But she also said, if he wanted to go on, he should find that little boy, the essence of George, and use him to gain strength and come back to them; whichever route he chose would be ok with them. She worked at this again and again, each time she sat with George, trying to reach him in some way. Rationally, she knew it was bonkers, but emotionally it felt absolutely the right thing to do.

For a few days they were convinced they had lost him, each person preparing his or herself for the worst. They began to think about his funeral, whether it would be a religious ceremony or not. It was hard, it was sad, but it seemed inevitable now. They kept the rest of the family informed by telephone and everyone waited in anticipation of the news that was sure to come. Imagine their confusion and surprise when, after a few days, he began to come round a little, and after a while gradually started to drink a little more and then to eat a small amount. And then one morning, as if nothing had happened, he simply asked the nurses from the PONT to open the curtains. He was clearly recovering. Everyone was stunned.

Mum and Dad spoke to Melanie who thought he had probably suffered some kind of brainstorm – a cerebrospinal fluid leak – from the effect of the tumour at the back of his throat, which was probably now growing into the base of his brain. They learnt that these kinds of incidents often happened and some families went through the grieving process two or three times, before the child finally passed away. Their hearts sank.

During the time that George was lying in the dark, Louis had stayed away from his room. He was having a hard time dealing with it all. Mum became concerned that if George died Louis would feel guilty and so she devised a way to get him to have some contact, however small. She would ask him to take in a cup of tea or some such thing for Dad or Despina and, while Louis was in the room, once George began to drift in and out of sleep, his younger brother would say hello. In this way, the spell was broken and Louis felt he could enter the 'forbidden zone'. As the weeks passed, he would sit with George watching a TV programme or just pop into his room after school to say "hi" or "how are you feeling?" Mum knew that sometimes he couldn't face seeing George in pain, seeing him suffering, not knowing what to say to make it ok, so he stayed away until the worst had passed. But that was ok. George understood it was hard for him; he was a good brother like that. They all knew it was a huge weight for a boy of twelve to carry.

Despina, who was now teaching in a primary school, took a week off work to be with George. She had already spent the Christmas holidays going to sleep at nights on the sofa bed downstairs, waking each morning and waiting for the sound of her father sobbing, the signal that would let her know George had gone. But the sobs never came and George started to improve. Every day for that week off, she would travel to the house and bring George something small to entice him to eat – a milkshake, a yoghurt, whatever little treat she could think of. Each day, they would watch a film together and chat, or she would encourage him to do eye exercises, foot exercises, massage his forehead.

At the end of the week, he said, "What am I going to do next week when you're not here?"

It broke her heart, but it was good to know how much he liked her to be with him. And she loved being there for him too. She had loved their little excursions to Costa, when he had been well enough to walk. Now they would no longer do those things and it hurt; she raged at the unfairness of it all.

And so they moved into a new phase, with George now bedridden and receiving pain relief by infusion and from patches on his arm. Despite his condition, he had not yet given up on the idea of being able to get out of bed and travel into Kingston for coffee with Louis and Despina. He kept a determined focus on his aim, but was struggling to take the necessary steps towards achieving it, too weak in reality to even get out of bed. He was becoming depressed at his lack of progress and so the counsellor from the Marsden began home visits and prescribed an anti-depressant. She presented him with a simple choice between medication that would be taken in the morning and give him more energy or a drug to be taken at night, which would also help him sleep. Given his record of insomnia during his illness and his worry that more energy might equal more frustration at not being able to get up and move around, George opted for the night time medication – Amitriptyline. This turned out to be a critical mistake. The medication appeared to make George foggy and more nauseous, and Dad worried that, in addition, this type of drug had the potential to accelerate tumour growth. Eventually George decided to stop taking the anti-depressant, as it seemed to make little difference to his mood and he felt it was affecting his ability to stay alert.

As the weeks passed, he continued to suffer sickness, despite being prescribed strong anti-emetic medication, which would often send him to sleep. He was now permanently relying on enemas and starting to develop pain in his right eye once more. He could no longer travel to hospital, and so the infusions of zoledronic acid he had been started on couldn't be continued. Dad requested an oral prescription of a drug that he understood would have a similar effect and presented Melanie with research papers to support his assertions. However, after consulting with colleagues, Melanie refused, on the grounds of still not enough evidence to demonstrate its effectiveness.

Despite the apparent hopelessness of the situation, Mum and Dad were still trying to find treatments that would fight the disease. However, they were now caught up in the world of medical ethics. The doctors believed, from their vast experience, that George was going to die; their primary concern was to keep him symptom-free and comfortable for as long as possible, as well as free from anxiety. It was by no means desirable to have a distressed and frightened patient, and the pain medication also acted to keep him calm. As pain relief was increased regularly, it gradually caused George to sleep more during the day, eat and drink less and suffer more nausea and constipation. There was a delicate balance to be achieved, between alleviating his suffering from pain, but not exacerbating his other problems. Mum and Dad saw him getting weaker each day and felt that the medication was contributing to this. Yet, still there were episodes of acute, excruciating pain. In addition, his leg was swelling increasingly with water retention from the DVT, causing him a great deal of discomfort that the pain medication didn't alleviate. The worst of all, however, was the development of bedsores – pressure sores – which the pain relief didn't seem to even touch. Consequently, the pain caused by the sores was at times more troublesome to George than the symptoms of the cancer itself.

On occasions George managed to sit on the side of the bed with assistance from a physiotherapist, the nurses and Mum and Dad. He wanted to be able to stand up, but his weak frame would now not support him to do so without help. However, he was determined to work at it. During February he made several attempts, starting with sitting on the side of the bed and graduating to standing for about a minute with two people supporting him. It was a simple enough task for most people, but for George it was a big event, requiring a great deal of effort on his part and at least three helpers.

First of all, they would clear a good space around the bed. Then George would raise himself up on his elbows and manoeuvre his hips round towards the edge of the bed. After this exertion he would need to rest for a moment and allow the pain to recede. For the next stage, two people would take his arms and pull him gently to a sitting position. He would then begin to push himself up off the bed, while the two helpers lifted him under his arms. At least one additional person was required to move the medication-dispensing pump and the urine bag and to keep the lines connected to these free from snagging and from being pulled out of his body. Once standing (he was completely naked, as he now found clothes of any kind were uncomfortable) he would be supported for a while, allowing him to take a little of his own weight. After a minute or so, he would state he had had enough and it would be time to reverse the process step by step and enable him to lie down again – exhausted. There would be declarations of well done all round. It was progress of a sort. He would take time to recover, have a sleep and try again in a few days.

"How the hell did we get here, Dad?" asked George.

Meanwhile his right eye began to cause more pain and to once again develop light sensitivity. It was also weeping and one morning there was a small amount of blood, which caused George to panic. As the days passed, there was a good deal of swelling and the eye began to protrude. By now, he had little movement in the eye and it was unclear how much he could actually see out of it. Melanie prescribed a course of dexamethasone, which helped for a while, but soon the problem began to increase once more. He became worried about losing his sight. Then, on Wednesday 9th February 2011, Melanie visited and Mum and Dad were warned that the eye could be pushed out completely. The potential for suffering seemed endless and Mum and Dad were overwhelmed.

That day, a doctor from Norfolk, who Dad had been in touch with for some time, was also visiting.

Henry Mannings, a doctor from the oncology clinic at James Paget Hospital, ran a small charity with its own treatment clinic and drop-in centre, called Star Throwers. The charity aimed to help late-stage cancer patients, for whom standard treatments had failed. Henry had been trying for some months to get permission to treat George with something called 'Coley's Vaccine'.

William Coley was a surgeon in nineteenth century United States, who discovered that patients whose wounds became infected post-surgery, and who did not die from the infection, would occasionally go into spontaneous remission – that is, the cancer would disappear. He realised that the infection was causing a reaction in the patient's immune system, enabling it to recognise and kill the cancer. He began work on developing a vaccine designed to stimulate such a reaction in cancer patients, and this was used as a cancer treatment for some time. It would provoke high temperatures in the patient, causing shivering and shaking, followed by the usual burning and fever that accompanies an acute rise in temperature. The treatment was given repeatedly over a number of weeks and was not a comfortable experience for the patient. After the invention of radiotherapy, Coley's Vaccine was abandoned.

Henry believed that the vaccine offered possibilities for treating cancer patients for whom all other treatments had failed. It had taken more than a year for him to get permission to treat George, who was still a minor. Now that he had finally received permission, George was in a very vulnerable state and Henry was concerned about treating him at all. The treatment was harsh and could weaken George further, but Dad was desperate to try to save his son and George was keen to proceed, especially after meeting Henry, who made quite an impression.

Henry was a quietly-spoken, warm, caring and emotional man of medium height and in late middle age, with short, tightly curled, fair to greying hair. He always looked people in the eye and spoke his mind, but also had a slightly distracted air about him, as if his mind was busy in the background with reflecting, sorting, assessing. Consequently, he could appear to be in another world or dithering, when he was doing nothing of the sort. He was intensely driven to help people and finally agreed to do what he could for George. He left with a promise to return ten days later with his head nurse, in order to teach Dad to administer the vaccine. In the meantime, before the treatment could commence, the family needed to identify a nurse to insert a cannula in George's hand – once a week for each five-day treatment period.

After Henry and the family had had discussions with Melanie and their oncologist, it was clear that neither of the latter were in a position to support the administering of the vaccine. They viewed the treatment as experimental and appeared to feel it would be unethical for them to be involved. Neither were the nurses from the PONT able to help, as they took their orders from Melanie. The only option was to find a nursing agency that would take on the task. The family paid a nurse to come out one day per week to carry out the procedure and to sit with George afterwards.

All this time, George was getting weaker; he couldn't turn himself in bed or sit up properly; and he was worrying about his eye. Then, one weekday morning, during a visit from the PONT, he began to talk to one of the nurses about dying. Following this, the same day, he discussed the issue with the counsellor, and that evening he requested time to speak to Dad alone. He began to voice his feelings about a subject that Mum and Dad had dreaded arising. Afterwards, he called for Mum to join them and repeated his thoughts and feelings for her. He was seventeen and facing the possibility of his own death. To his parents, the world had never seemed so cruel.

George said that he knew it could happen now, although he hastened to add that it might not of course.

He said, "The hardest thing will be leaving you all because I love you so much."

He was very afraid of what it would be like. Dad assured him that they would be there with him, holding him. Mum told him she had heard that when people were really ill and exhausted, they became detached from the world and those close to them and felt ready to leave in a way that the rest of us cannot comprehend. He said that he too felt removed at times and so perhaps it was already happening to him. However, he was quick to say that he felt it could go either way. Later, he spoke to his sister and his brother too.

It was the one and only time George spoke of death. Once he had voiced his feelings, he made it clear that he preferred to get on with attempting to live. It was upsetting and draining for all concerned, but at the same time they had to admit there was a certain feeling of relief to have broached the subject that was obviously in everyone's mind. George had done all the work for them, but it was hard to gauge how afraid he actually was. He clearly didn't wish to dwell on the issue and they followed his lead. Whether from respect for his wishes or from their own fears about dwelling on the subject, it was never mentioned again.

Around this time, the sixth form at George's school asked him to nominate a charity to be the beneficiary of their rag week activities. He chose Star Throwers, as a show of gratitude to Henry and all he had tried to do, and so that others might continue to benefit from their work.

Then it was February half term. Mum and Louis drove up to visit Nanny Olive for the weekend. To their dismay, they had another nine-hour journey; this time the catalytic converter fell out of the engine on the busy A12 in the pouring rain. They began to wonder if they were jinxed.

Meanwhile, Dad, Despina and George spent time at home. They ordered takeaways, watched films and chatted together. It was a good three days for them, happy together, like old times when it had just been the three of them. George's condition seemed to be stabilising at last and he was talking about getting up again, working towards being able to walk, or even taking up his driving lessons again. Dad was mixing up potions of liposomal quercetin and curcumin, which luckily didn't taste too bad and which George took twice a day without complaint. Dad was mostly putting on a brave face, but for a few days even he began to feel that it was possible George had turned a corner.

Mum and Louis passed a pleasant weekend, getting plenty of sea air walking Flash along the beach and watching the waves crashing down in the blustery weather. But it was unnerving being away from George and Dad. So much had been happening to George that they were never quite sure if he would take a sudden turn for the worse.

Mum sent George a text and asked how he was doing. The reply was upsetting; he wanted to stand up again. It was so totally frustrating and he seemed overwhelmed with emotion – with anger and the feeling of failure. He said he wasn't making any headway in moving towards the target he had set. He felt the PONT weren't supporting him to move forward and he couldn't understand why. Mum sent a text back, saying if he wanted to stand up, then that's exactly what they would do as soon as she and Louis returned home. Not to worry, they could do it without the nurses sometimes – with Mum, Dad and Despina or Louis. It seemed to calm him a little.

On returning home they did help George to stand again. It was such a tiny thing for a human being to achieve and yet such an enormous task for him, requiring the use of all the energy and determination he could muster. It was a far cry from his goal of going into Kingston to have coffee with Despina and Louis, but Mum and Dad knew he would never make that journey now – unless there was a miracle of some kind.

Meanwhile, he still suffered daily bouts of vomiting, of pain in his hip and his swollen ankle, as well as intermittent pain in his eye. He had started on the Coley's vaccine, achieving moderately high temperatures after the first week or so, but after two or three weeks more it became clear that the vaccine was weakening George. It wasn't easy to watch someone so exhausted and ill becoming even more strained by the treatment. At the same time, the vaccine didn't seem to be achieving anything positive. The Coley's was at least expected to reduce bone tumour pain, but it seemed even this was not to be for George. Eventually, after a few weeks the decision was made to abandon the treatment. George was unhappy. Mum, Dad and Henry assured him he could try again once he was a little stronger if he concentrated on building himself up first; but they knew it was a lie – permission to give the treatment had come too late.

George was dying; it was the end of the line. It was only a matter of how much time and how much suffering. The swelling in his right eye, which had been reduced temporarily, was now increasing again. There was little movement in the eye and George didn't seem able to see out of it. In addition, his left eye began to cause him pain and he became anxious about losing his sight completely. He was often confused and sleepy with the cocktail of pain and anti-sickness medication, while the pressure sores were becoming excruciatingly painful. Although he had already been provided with a hospital bed, in the hopes of alleviating some of the suffering from the sores, he was given a new bed with an expensive, memory foam mattress. Transferring him from the old to the new bed took several people, as any sudden movement could provoke an episode of acute pain in the pelvic tumour or the sores. But the new mattress helped a little, as did the lamb's wool fleece that Dad had ordered to place under his back. The single most effective relief however seemed to come from the medical grade Manuka honey, which Dad bought and convinced the PONT nurses to apply under the dressings. But despite everything they did to try and help, the pressure sores would never heal properly.

And so George deteriorated over the next few weeks, gradually unable to stand or sit on the side of the bed, or move very much at all. Apart from odd occasions, when he became a little more alert and chatty, he slept for longer, ate less and suffered increased pain, which was met with increased medication. Mum made little attempts to cook small dishes that he fancied, Despina tried a few take-away items to tempt him, other family members brought him chocolates and similar easy to eat morsels, but it was clear that he could manage very little. His best friend came to see him but mostly he slept through the visits, rousing only to say goodbye and to apologise for being asleep.

Then he began to slur his speech and his hands began to shake, making manipulation of the simplest items very difficult. He abandoned the new, fancy phone he had purchased off the Internet, in favour of the old one with the buttons that were easier to press. The tumour at the base of the brain was the cause of the new symptoms, and it was this tumour that was to gradually cause him to close down and finally to stop breathing. It was the silent, invisible killer, unlike the tumour on the pelvis, which could be seen to increase in girth almost daily now – protruding aggressively from his skeletal frame. The bone-thin appearance of his left leg was accentuated by the hugely swollen right leg. His poor right eye protruded from its socket, as much as his face dipped on the other side from the missing temporalis muscle, while his right jaw was still swollen from his three operations. His once beautiful face, with the huge, brown, melting, mischievous eyes and the wide cheeky grin, was now completely distorted. The cancer had ravaged him.

Inside, he was still George. But when was the last time they had seen the 'real' George? The George whose sharp humour and little jokes made everyone laugh? The George who had posted on Facebook "Cancer is soooo anoyin, id advise against it lol." The George whose reckless, fearless, physical antics gave Mum and Dad so much concern? The smart George, who came up with clever ways to solve a maths equation and discussed the latest on robots and artificial intelligence with his dad? The competitive teenager? The stubborn, supremely confident boy? The brother who took great delight in winding up his younger sibling, who was the only one able to tell Despina to just calm down at times of stress? Who was laid back and cool and smiling and loving and caring? That George was fading away from them.

In the last weeks, there were increasingly long gaps between his loud, rasping snatches of breath. Whoever was sitting with George would hold his or her own breath, listening to see if the boy would inhale again at all. He or she would rush to the bedside and call George's name, letting out a loud sigh of relief as the laboured intake of breath suddenly began again. But it was simply that he had forgotten to breathe for a minute, as the tumour at the base of the skull interfered with the normally automatic action of respiration. Over and over again these false alarms happened as the final weeks and then days passed by.

Easter holidays came and Despina arrived one morning. George was no longer able to clean his teeth without assistance. As she helped him manipulate the electric toothbrush, she realised he was in such a bad way that he couldn't even manage to spit out the toothpaste.

She watched films with him and when he kept falling asleep, she turned the film off and told him to rest.

He replied, "Ok, but don't go anywhere, stay here with me." She cried then, knowing he must have been scared, wondering if he knew there was a possibility he wouldn't wake up.

What it is to anticipate the loss of a loved one, to await the inevitable, at times willing the arrival of the event, in order that the suffering should stop; at the same time, to dread the finality, the 'no more', the 'gone'. It was surely a form of torture.

And then finally it came, on a Sunday night in late April. For 24 hours George had hardly emerged from his deep sleep, and even then only to briefly open his eyes. He was no longer able to eat and finally not even to take a sip of water. He stayed in an almost-coma, unrousable and snatching long, harsh, irregular breaths. Dad didn't leave his side, but sat with the tears streaming down his face, as he spoke quietly to George and stroked his head. He told him how much he loved him, that he was there by his side and wouldn't leave him.

Despina was afraid and couldn't face being in the house any longer, but at the same time was anxious about leaving for the night. She had lost her mother at the age of eight and now she was on the verge of losing her brother, her friend. Dad could see how tired she was and, reassuring her, he told her to go home and get some sleep; if anything happened he would contact her. She said her goodbyes, poured out everything she needed to say to George and left. She went to Tom's for the night, but she didn't sleep: she was sick and spent the rest of the night waiting for a phone call from Dad.

Louis came in to sit with George. He sat still and silent next to the bed, watching his brother slipping away from him.

Then, in the silence, came Louis's words "I love you mate" and the sound of his choked-back tears. He was 12 years old, watching his 17-year-old brother dying.

Mum sat and stroked George's head. It was hard to tell just how long he would last. They had already seen him recover from a near coma and Mum felt he might well do it again. But Dad knew. And so, when Mum finally went to snatch a few hours sleep at around 1.30 in the morning, Dad stayed sitting next to George, holding his hand, stroking his head, whispering words of love and comfort. Mum saw how exhausted Dad looked and placed some cushions on the floor next to the bed. Dad lay down to doze for a couple of hours. He would have liked to sleep on the bed next to George, but it was impossible; any movement could disturb the medication pump or cause pain to the pelvis. It hadn't even been possible to hold George properly for some months. And so, exhausted, he lay down on the cushions for a while.

At 3.47 a.m. on Monday 25th April 2011 George let out his last long breath, arousing Dad as he did so. He had slipped away quietly, with no fuss. Dad rushed to his side, the grief coming fast and strong as he realised that his lovely boy had finally gone.

He stroked his head, the tears falling on to his son's face, as he repeated over and over, "I'm sorry

Georgie, I'm so sorry."

He rushed in to wake Mum and the two of them sat quietly for a while, watching the absent boy – still there, but not there.

At 4.15 a.m. they rang the PONT and informed them of George's passing. Dad rang Despina and told her; Mum could hear her sobbing down the phone, although later she said she was screaming, as no tears would come until she reached the house. Then, at 7.00 a.m. Mum and Dad woke Louis and told him George had passed away. They sat on his bed and held the sobbing boy close, the pain of their loss increased by the pain of his loss.

The PONT dealt with all the complications and arrangements, and the rest of the morning passed in a numb haze. There was an awful period when they couldn't reach George's GP to come and confirm cause of death and, as a result, the coroner was insisting on an autopsy. Fortunately they managed to contact the other family GP, who had kindly left her mobile number with Dad; she came and signed the death certificate. George was at least allowed some dignity in death, if such a thing is possible.

They helped the nurses wash and dress George's body, choosing one of his favourite shirts, but only loose jogging bottoms for his legs, concerned even in death for his comfort. They pulled socks over his feet, over the swollen ankle on his right leg. They arranged him comfortably and pulled the sheet back over him.

Finally, the time came for George to be taken out. He was to be conveyed to the local children's hospice, where he would be laid out. The undertakers arrived, quiet and respectful, but business-like, and set about their task. They carried George's body down the stairs and out to the waiting ambulance. As they did so, harsh reality hit home again: it was the hardest thing – George was gone.

For The Love of George

16. After George's Passing

It was a sunny, warm April day when George died, the blue sky and bright sunshine belying the sad emptiness felt by the family. The world roused itself as normal and life went about its daily business. People walked briskly to work, took the bus, ran for the train. Dogs were taken for their constitutional in the early morning air. Young children trotted along beside their parents heading for the local primary school, or whizzed ahead on scooters, taking care to stop at the roads as they had been taught. The girls from the sixth form of the school next door chatted and laughed in small groups as they passed by the front of the house, exchanging notes perhaps on the weekend's events or a project set by a long-standing teacher. Cars were started, buses crawled along in the Monday morning traffic.

In the days and weeks that followed, Mum began to wonder what was going on behind the seemingly normal faces that she passed in the street. Were there others out there who were experiencing sadness, pain, grief? Others who were moving about the world in a dream, with a strange sense of unreality, one removed from everything around them? Of course there were. You never knew who they were as you passed them in the street.

It was after midday on the day of George's passing that Dad, Mum, Despina and Louis set off in their unreal world, to make their unreal journey to the hospice where his body was laid out. They drove in silence, apart from small exchanges about when to turn left or right, and at around 12.30 p.m. they pulled into the Sainsbury's car park next to the hospice. They rang the bell at the solid wooden gate that was set in the high walls, announcing to the intercom that they were George Pantziarka's family, knowing they were expected, that today they were special. They were invited in and taken through reception, past the hall on the left, with the kitchen on the right, and down the corridor to 'the door'. They had never been into the room that lay behind it. This was the door that Dad had refused to go through when they were first shown around the hospice. On it was a plaque with the simple title 'Tranquil Suite'. A member of staff unlocked it and they were shown in.

Inside, another unreal, unfamiliar world was waiting for them. They stepped into a small entrance hall, to the left of which they saw a room furnished with comfortable chairs and calming paintings and a table scattered with leaflets – a room for reflection, a sort of religious room they guessed. Ahead was a sitting room with a sofa and some chairs and a book of remembrance on a small table. There were flowers placed around the room, which was decorated in peaceful pastels. To the left were large glass doors, leading out to a small walled garden – a Secret Garden for grieving families. To the right was another door, which was being unlocked for them. In here, George was laid out.

They put on their jumpers against the cold they knew would lie within and they entered together. The windowless room was dimly lit and an icy chill hit them in the face. Before leaving the house, they had gathered up some of George's possessions and they now placed these around him in the room, in a vain attempt to make the formal, icy atmosphere more personal. Did they want to pretend that George was really just lying in bed, asleep, still there, still present? And yet it was as if he was still present. He was still George – just very cold, very still, George.

Louis, face-to-face with death in a way most children in this country do not find themselves, touched George's forehead; they all did in their own time. Louis felt the ice-cold; that was a shock, it didn't feel like George. And then the tears came, in floods. Mum and Dad held Louis close. Dad held his only daughter, 25 years old, but still a little girl inside, who had lost her mum to cancer at the age of eight; and now, her brother.

The room was stark, but there was a small lamp on the bedside table where they had laid some of George's belongings – his Manga art and film animation books, one of his many hats – the pink and grey striped one with the long plaits hanging down either side that he had worn so often – his watch, his mobile phone that was so much part of who he was. On another table opposite the end of the bed they placed the small shield he had gained as an award from school, for 'endeavour leading to achievement'. There was the ceramic elephant that had belonged to his mother before she had died, and the chopsticks he had brought back from China. All these things proclaimed different aspects of George's life, his character.

George had been tucked into the bed, with the covers pulled up to his neck. It really was almost as if he were just in his bed, sleeping; but cold. His head was turned slightly to one side. They had placed him so that you couldn't see the bad side of his face so much, the side where he had had three operations to reconstruct his jaw.

After a while, Louis left the room with his sister; Mum followed; Dad came a little after. Dad and Louis sat on the sofa in the sitting room; Despina sat outside on the bench, staring into space, desolate, bereft. Mum was overcome with pity at the sight of her. She went and sat next to her and put her arm round her. They had never seen eye to eye, never really enjoyed each other's company. That was putting it mildly. But that morning, when Despina had arrived at the house, she had tried to communicate with Mum, to make peace, sitting on the sofa in George's room together, staring at his dead body. And Mum felt ashamed that this young woman, thirty years her junior, had been the one to make the move. So now she tried to comfort Despina and say things to ease the pain. They stayed like this until Dad and Louis came and joined them, all four sitting in the garden, with the little silver stars of remembrance, bearing the names of lost children, twinkling in the sunlight where they hung from the tree in the centre.

The members of staff at the hospice were kind and considerate. They brought a tray of tea and biscuits; they explained that the family had use of the suite as long as they required and that lunch was available to them if they wanted. And so they sat and drank the tea and nibbled the biscuits absentmindedly, making small attempts at conversation. Then they ordered some lunch and ate in the dining room. Some children who were resident at the hospice were also taking their lunch at another table, assisted by members of staff, their liveliness contrasted with the limp lethargy of the family. After lunch they left, driving home in the sunny afternoon with one child fewer than the day before.

In the days that followed, they made preparations for George's funeral. Mum, Dad, Despina and Louis had decided it should be a non-religious affair, as George wasn't religious – although others would be free to speak religious words around his grave. Accordingly, in the days after the funeral, Yiayia and Buppou would bring a Greek Orthodox priest to the graveside to carry out a small ceremony. And it was arranged that George would be buried in the same grave as his mother, in the plot that had originally been purchased for husband and wife to share – no one imagining that the child would pass before the parent.

The family contacted George's closest friends

and asked them to speak at the funeral and one of his friends was asked to read a piece of George's writing. Dad wrote a speech, but asked Mum to deliver it. Dad and Despina chose two of his favourite pieces of music. Despina and Louis put together the programme to be given out to those attending on the day. George's cousin, Penny was to speak at the graveside. Uncle David and George's best friend were to be pallbearers. After the service, Louis was to hand over the cheque from the rag week collection, to Henry, in George's name. George's old school friends put together a display of the tributes that had been left on Facebook, and an old primary school friend delivered a booklet that she had made for George, with contributions from several young people about the good times they had all had together. The family chose photographs of George going back to when he was a young boy, to add to the display. Mum's friends looked after the refreshments that would be provided in the cemetery – bread and wine in Greek Orthodox tradition, plus other bits and pieces provided by Yiayia and Buppou. It was a joint effort, a pulling together by those figuring large and small in the life of George. The family were pleased that those who attended said it felt very personal, "very George."

The funeral service took place in the small chapel at the cemetery. The family dressed smartly for the occasion in honour of George. Even Louis was wearing a black suit and smart shoes. They waited nervously for the funeral cars to arrive at the house to pick them up. In the middle of the awfulness, Dad had a little rant about climate change and the 'hysterical warmists' – the believers in catastrophic man-made global warming. Mum was glad; it kept him going. But still, the sight of the hearse was too much for him and for Yiayia and they both broke down.

When they approached the chapel in the funeral cars, down the long lane running through the cemetery, they were overwhelmed by the sight of the huge crowd of people standing outside – a sea of faces, of family, friends, George's friends, the PONT, the palliative care team, Mum's and Dad's work colleagues, teachers and many, many young people, not only from the sixth forms he had attended, but young people who had been at primary school with George. The word had spread; Facebook had done its work. The small chapel was overflowing. And it was a comfort for which the family was grateful. So much support, so many kind words, wonderful messages, tributes, cards, flowers. In a small way, it all helped. Speeches were given, music was played and there was a ripple of emotion as the words "this is goodbye" rang out from a Moby song, in the small chapel.

After the funeral, the close family went back to the house for a couple of hours. The dog walker, who had lost her sister to cancer a couple of years before, returned Flash, whom she had kept for two long walks. People drank tea and chatted, until finally, by 5.00 p.m. everyone was gone. Mum and Dad went to lie down, tired out, empty. Louis went to his room to relax. Despina returned to her flat to be comforted by Tom.

Later it was parents' consultation evening for

Louis in his first year at George's old school. Mum decided to go along with Louis – more cards and words of support. As they entered the school, they stopped to look at the photograph of George playing football, which was mounted on the wall in the foyer. He was young, fresh, happy and full of life in the photo; it was good to see it. They hoped it would always remain there.

And so the first days went by. Louis returned to school the following week, Despina returned to work, Dad spent two weeks at home with Mum. They walked the dog in the countryside, talked a lot and he tried to prepare himself mentally for his return to work. Mum had no idea what she was going to do now that her PhD was completed. Flash made his way up to George's room occasionally, as if searching for the company of his old friend.

They went to the supermarket, cooked dinner, walked the dog, hoovered the house, played on the Xbox, went to work, went to school, dealt with paperwork and understood that life continued. They visited George's grave, spent time in his room; they cried. Time passed.

17. The Only Game in Town

In the first weeks following George's death, Louis kept remembering little incidents – some comic, some just everyday things – such as when they had walked the dog together, or had been at a family gathering. He decided to collect his memories, making a note of them on his mobile. Facebook too was a comfort to him – reading the many messages posted about George, responding with his own and taking responsibility for posting a couple of messages from Mum and Dad. His cousins would regularly post on Facebook and it was good to know the family were there. But there were also bad days, when he would return from school wanting to tell George something that had happened, and the sudden memory that his brother was no longer there would stop him short. He would be caught out by those moments, when we think "oh yes, I'll tell so and so about that…"

At one point he panicked that he hadn't told George he loved him, until he remembered the last night

297

of George's life, when he had sat by the bed – "I love you mate." It had been important for him to settle things, for George to know how he felt about him – a difficult thing to negotiate and the last thing they would ever have said to each other under normal circumstances.

Dad was to be tortured again and again by the knowledge that he had been unable to save his son and was forever agonising over whether the decisions he had made were right or wrong. Why did they do such and such? What if they had done something else instead? And he and Mum were tortured by the wrong decisions others had made. If only they had done this instead of that... It was useless to rake over the coals in this way. They had all made mistakes, but there is little chance that George would have survived. The statistics they had so boldly turned away from in those first weeks of his illness proved the case. And the oncologists had known it. And yet, should one just give up in the face of adversity? How could they have done? It certainly wasn't George's way. There was always the possibility, the positive outcome that did happen for the few, even in the most unlikely circumstances. To give up hope was to give up on life.

And the loss – what is this thing called loss? How can it be that one moment we have someone with us, and the next they are gone? A split second's difference between that last exhalation and nothing more; a fine line that once crossed, can never be reversed. One moment he is here, the next he is gone; he is breathing, he is not breathing; he exists, he no longer exists – at least not in concrete terms. He exists in memory, in his belongings that still adorn his bedroom, in the photos displayed around the house, in the dreams that haunt Dad. He is a name, a relative, a friend, but he will never be physically, materially here again. He will never touch your hand again, laugh at your jokes, wrestle your arm, turn as he leaves the room and give that last broad smile, before disappearing upstairs.

Believers – those who have faith in a religion – find some comfort. They envisage their loved-ones moved on to some superior plane, to a world where their pain and suffering is no more, to a place where others can be reunited with them when they too pass on. Those who have more ephemeral beliefs, but not exactly religious, can take comfort in the thought that their loved one exists somehow in spirit, in the universal consciousness. But those who believe in the finality of material existence? Those who take the name atheist? What comfort do they have? No, there is no comfort here; the loved-one is lost and will never be found again, except in our memories and the items and rituals we endow with meaning, necessary to enable us to go on.

What can we do when we lose a child? Create something in their name? Purchase a bench, a tree or a plaque? Start a charity to help others in similar situations? Cherish their memory and learn from their example in the short life lived.

And the loss of day-to-day contact, of sharing, of holding? There is no substitute for that, not even for the religious amongst us. The terrible ache will continue, hopefully fading in time, as other life grows around it and other attachments are nurtured and thrive. Other children will be cherished, spouses will be held close and ease the gripping pain that produces the almost silent sobbing. The beauty and cruelty of life will sit side by side in the now unfathomable world.

The beauty of early morning mist clinging to the trees, with the sun poking dimly through, while Flash bounds over the forest floor, chasing a squirrel in complete abandonment. The sound of waves crashing on a deserted beach, under a blue sky punctuated by fluffy white clouds. A field of wild flowers swaying gently in a warm breeze. Life goes on.

Dad manages to laugh and engage with life for some of the time and he's kept busy by an ever-demanding job. Mum says it's a case of joining up the dots, until the good things in life grow and fill your world. It's not that the pain can be obliterated, but other parts of life can grow around it. She has hope for their future together.

The first week passes, first month, first birthday, first summer holiday, first Christmas. First anniversary. Mum waiting to get past the first year, so that perhaps every little event will not take on such significance, echoing the absence of George. But when they reach that milestone, it's an anti-climax. There is no great catharsis, no sense of freedom. Friends post on Facebook – missing George, an inspiration to them, the strongest person they ever knew. The day is charged, but still just another day without George. It is also frightening to step into the territory of the second year, beyond the safety net of the early days, when everyone understands that it is difficult and sympathises accordingly. Time has moved so fast and now it's on with 'real life'. Now there is only what they make of things, how they actively shape their own future from this moment.

As time goes on, the acuteness of the loss recedes. What is left is a chronic ache, which gets worse. There is the fear of forgetting how George sounded, how he laughed, the fear that he will just be forgotten, that it will be as if he never existed. It is a strange unknown territory to be negotiated. The finality of his passing dawns again and again and Dad misses George more and more. That is what has to be dealt with now. But it makes no more sense as time goes on. It is still inconceivable that George no longer exists. It is the oddest thing – he was, and now he is no more.

There is a weight, a heaviness to life now that Mum feels constantly. She can enjoy things each day, laugh with Dad and Louis, take pleasure in tending her garden, growing fruit and veg in the small suburban plot, watching the butterflies, bees, dragonflies flitting and buzzing around. But there is always a film playing in the background. It replays events, gives a constant reminder of death, of her own mortality; it is a kind of white noise that repeats the question, "why?" Dad has the same sensation, a constant backdrop of George and his suffering. Even Louis relates to this view of life now. They live these two lives at once. Life is beautiful; life is cruel and meaningless. Ours is not to reason why…

Despina announces her engagement to Tom. He

is the man for her; he knows, he understands what she has been through. He knew her brother and George liked him. She couldn't marry someone who hadn't been part of it all. The wedding is planned and everyone is happy for her; and everyone feels sadness that George will not be there – especially Despina.

The family feels the need to do something worthwhile in George's name to help others fight this terrible disease. They set up a charity for Li Fraumeni Syndrome sufferers. Dad sets up the Anti-Cancer website (http://www.anticancer.org.uk/) that he and George had discussed, for which George had already designed the logo. George's school names a prize in his honour, to be given annually to a boy who carries on in the face of adversity, as uncomplaining as George was. Mum, Dad and Louis attend the prize-giving and Dad presents the prize to a young lad who beams brightly in response. At the same prize-giving Louis steps up on to the stage to receive the very prize that George was awarded. It is a moment of pride as they read the family name now engraved on the two big shields for key stages three and four. His sister applies for a job teaching in a children's cancer unit. Cousin Penny is accepted on to the youth advisory team of Cancer Research UK. Mum writes. George's name lives on and means something. Yet, we are here and he is not.

Life goes on. What choice do we have but to go on too, for as long as we are here? We have been granted what George was denied. We build new lives, we plan new adventures, look to our futures. We continue to search for some meaning, some knowledge that surpasses our understanding so far. But, even in its absence, we go on with life.

After all, it's the only game in town.

For The Love of George

Postscript

The George Pantziarka TP53 Trust is a registered charity established by George's parents following his death in April 2011. The Trust exists to support individuals and families afflicted by Li Fraumeni Syndrome (LFS) or related conditions – the same genetic syndrome that affected George and which led to him developing three different cancers in his short life.

The charity provides support and advice, publishes a website with a forum and supports on-going research into this rare condition. Much current research on LFS is focused on understanding the complex genetics of the syndrome or on establishing new surveillance protocols to catch and treat cancer early. A key aim of the Trust is to move beyond this approach and to encourage, and fund, research that looks at active means to stop cancer developing in

For The Love of George

the first place. Genes should not equal destiny, even in a condition like LFS.

It is the only organisation in the UK dedicated to LFS and needs support from the public in carrying out its work. A portion of the proceeds of this book will go to the Trust, but you can do more and donate directly online at

https://mydonate.bt.com/charities/georgepantziarkat p53trust

To find out more about the work of the Trust, please visit http://www.tp53.co.uk or find us on Facebook.

George Pantziarka TP53 Trust

Made in the USA
Columbia, SC
05 May 2017